T0353609

AI FOR THE SUSTAINABLE DEVELOPMENT GOALS

AI FOR EVERYTHING

Artificial intelligence (AI) is all around us. From driverless cars to game-winning computers to fraud protection, AI is already involved in many aspects of life, and its impact will only continue to grow in future. Many of the world's most valuable companies are investing heavily in AI research and development, and not a day goes by without news of cutting-edge breakthroughs in AI and robotics.

The *AI for Everything* series will explore the role of AI in contemporary life, from cars and aircraft to medicine, education, fashion, and beyond. Concise and accessible, each book is written by an expert in the field and will bring the study and reality of AI to a broad readership including interested professionals, students, researchers, and lay readers.

AI for Immunology
Louis J. Catania

AI for Cars
Josep Aulinas & Hanky Sjafrie

AI for Digital Warfare
Niklas Hageback & Daniel Hedblom

AI for Art
Niklas Hageback & Daniel Hedblom

AI for Creativity
Niklas Hageback

AI for Death and Dying
Maggi Savin-Baden

AI for Radiology
Oge Marques

AI for Games
Ian Millington

AI for School Teachers
Rose Luckin. Karine George & Mutlu Cukurova

AI for Learners
Carmel Kent & Benedict du Boulay

AI for Social Justice
Alan Dix and Clara Crivellaro

AI for the Sustainable Development Goals
Henrik Skaug Sætra

For more information about this series please visit:
https://www.routledge.com/AI-for-Everything/book-series/AIFE

AI FOR THE SUSTAINABLE DEVELOPMENT GOALS

HENRIK SKAUG SÆTRA

CRC Press
Taylor & Francis Group
Boca Raton London New York

CRC Press is an imprint of the
Taylor & Francis Group, an **informa** business

First Edition published 2022
by CRC Press
6000 Broken Sound Parkway NW, Suite 300, Boca Raton, FL 33487-2742

and by CRC Press
4 Park Square, Milton Park, Abingdon, Oxon, OX14 4RN

CRC Press is an imprint of Taylor & Francis Group, LLC

Library of Congress Cataloging-in-Publication Data
Names: Sætra, Henrik Skaug, author.
Title: AI for the sustainable development goals / Henrik Skaug Sætra.
Description: Boca Raton : CRC Press, 2022. | Series: AI for everything |
Includes bibliographical references and index.
Identifiers: LCCN 2021044475 | ISBN 9781032044378 (hardback) |
ISBN 9781032044064 (paperback) | ISBN 9781003193180 (ebook)
Subjects: LCSH: Sustainable Development Goals. |
Sustainable development. | Artificial intelligence.
Classification: LCC HC79.E5 S2187 2022 | DDC 338.9/27—dc23
LC record available at https://lccn.loc.gov/2021044475

ISBN: 978-1-032-04437-8 (hbk)
ISBN: 978-1-032-04406-4 (pbk)
ISBN: 978-1-003-19318-0 (ebk)

DOI: 10.1201/9781003193180

Typeset in Joanna
by codeMantra

CONTENTS

Contents

AUTHOR

Henrik Skaug Sætra is an associate professor at the Faculty of Computer Science, Engineering and Economics at Østfold University College. He is a political scientist with a broad and interdisciplinary approach to issues of ethics and the individual, societal, and environmental implications of technology, environmental ethics, and game theory. Sætra has in recent years worked extensively on the effects of technology on liberty and autonomy and on various issues related to the use of social robots.

1

INTRODUCTION

Who would have thought that applied statistics and pattern recognition would have given rise to a phenomenon that is today described both as one of the greatest threats *and* hopes for human society? Artificial intelligence (AI) has been established as a key technology for solving modern challenges in business, politics, and also in our personal lives. While AI is seemingly conquering new markets, sectors, and problems every day, some are deeply concerned about the negative consequences it produces. In terms of challenges and threats to our societies, few frameworks communicate their broad and fundamental character better than the idea of *sustainable development*, which is today often related to the United Nation's (2015) Sustainable Development Goals (SDGs). These goals were launched in 2015 as part of Agenda 2030, and they encompass 17 goals focused on environmental goals, goals related to social justice, and goals related to economic growth, health, work, and politics.

The basic idea of sustainable development – that we must strive to satisfy our needs today without jeopardizing the needs of future generations – has garnered increasing attention since it was developed by the Brundtland commission in 1987 (Brundtland, Khalid, Agnelli, Al-Athel, & Chidzero, 1987). Particularly so, since we are daily getting new reports that show how humans are incontrovertibly changing and affecting their environment in problematic ways.

DOI: 10.1201/9781003193180-1

Much attention is devoted to the climate, increasing temperatures and more climate instability, the loss of species and decreased bio-diversity, and various forms of pollution, for example, the vast amounts of plastic in our oceans. This is the environmental dimension of sustainability. However, sustainable development as a concept also encompasses the social and economic dimensions, which detail how issues of justice, distribution, and the way we create economic growth are intimately linked to how we affect the potential of future generations.

How did I end up discussing justice, economic growth, and the climate when the importance of AI was my subject? The increasing power of AI systems has led to their ubiquity, and as already mentioned, AI is increasingly heralded as the enabler of a better future. This book scrutinizes this argument by analyzing how AI can enable and prevent the achievement of the SDGs.

The positive potential of AI to help or hinder the achievement of the SDGs is too great to be neglected. However, it is easy to be dazzled by the sunshine stories of AI success, while being blinded to the fact that AI might simultaneously be an inhibitor. The dual nature of AI sustainability and the challenge of getting to grips with AI impacts, will be the focus of the rest of this book. For example, I am one of those who like having smart devices, such as a smartwatch and a smartphone. This enables me to keep track of a vast array of aspects related to both health and fitness, and the more I use these devices, the more helpful they become as data is gathered and AI is used to analyze and provide me with personalized suggestions for activities that will most benefit me and my health. This must clearly have a positive impact on AI, right, as SDG 3 is about good health? Superficially, yes, but the real impact might not be particularly large, or even positive. First of all, the impact might not be that strong. In addition, when you add the fact that such use of AI entails producing new sorts of equipment, using energy and computing infrastructure to process my data and produce emissions, and how such technologies can increase the health gaps between those with the resources to purchase such equipment and those who do not, the positive impact could easily be argued to marginal at best. SDG 3, when one looks deeper into it, describes things such as universal health care, reduced maternal mortality rates, the death of newborns, and a particular focus on improving the health and well-being of those least well of. Helping me in Norway perform slightly better on my after-work run through increased consumption of gadgets and the generation of emissions does not seem to be the primary focus of the goal.

On a more general level, while AI might be used to make various systems more efficient, and thereby reducing their emissions, the data centers running these AI systems are increasing their emissions. AI might also be able to foster economic growth and the creation of jobs, but it will also be used to displace jobs, and perhaps also to automate recruitment interviews, and in the implementation of employer surveillance, etc. Another aspect related to economic growth and innovation is how the advances associated with AI systems could lead to increased inequalities between groups, countries, and regions. While the SDGs seem relatively simple at first sight, the 17 top-level goals actually consist of a large number of targets in which it becomes clear that growth in itself is not the goal – it has to be sustainable, equitable, and benefit all regardless of class, race, gender, etc. (United Nations, 2015).

Complicated indeed, and the purpose of this book is to present a method for evaluating and making sense of the various impacts of AI, and in particular how we should go about it to grasp the interdependence between the economic, social, and environmental dimensions of sustainability. In order to get to grips with both the short-term and long-term effects of AI systems, it is necessary to consider such systems in context, and not as some isolated and neutral tool (Sætra, 2021a). The AI systems examined in this book will be considered as parts of the sociotechnical system. This consists of various institutions, structures, and economic and political systems. These elements are all mutually dependent, each of the parts impacts the other parts, and they all enable, restrict, and shape the development and use of AI systems. And AI, in turn, impacts the other parts of the system.

An isolationist approach to technology stands in stark contrast to the one here outlined (Barley, 2020). Such an approach would allow us to, for example, run an experiment where we test the ability of an AI system to help guide city traffic. If successful, we might conclude that AI helps a number of goals, but in particular, the SDGs related to innovation and infrastructure. However, a non-isolationist approach demands that we take one step back and consider the development of the systems tested. Are they built on commonly available data sources? Are they proprietary systems? Do they require a level of computing power that is only available to a select few countries? Answering such questions is required for determining whether innovations become available to local communities and help reduce inequalities as required by the SDGs.

In the remainder of this book, you will be presented with a range of cases in which AI is indeed enabling sustainable development, and this is by no means meant to be an argument against AI. However, when we develop and deploy AI systems, we must do so on the basis of a realistic and balanced understanding of the positive and the negative implications of AI. This means asking fundamental questions related to fair and equitable access to these systems in addition to just how well these systems work their magic in particular use cases. It also means that we must consider the direct effects of these systems while also following through in order to properly assess the indirect effects. Of particular importance is how AI will have a major impact on SDG 9 which relates to innovation. Any success in achieving this goal will have important ripple effects for other goals. A proper understanding of how AI impacts the SDGs is facilitated by the approach used in this book, where the presence of ripple effects allows us to account for broad impacts without simply counting the same thing many times without endeavoring to understand the interlinkages between the impacts. Lastly, it is imperative to evaluate the *scale* of the impacts, instead of relying on a binary approach in which each success or failure is considered equal no matter how significant or insignificant it is. It is, for example, important to distinguish between an insignificant positive impact to reducing gender equality and a substantial contribution to the promotion of climate action. As you will see, achieving all these goals requires that we combine a range of sources of knowledge. Both experimental evidence and philosophical concerns will be addressed, as many of the long-term and broader implications of AI are not readily available for empirical observation. Some of the impacts are thus relatively certain, while others are more or less probable. This is, however, not a problem, but rather an intrinsic part of any social scientific project in which the scope is as broad as this book's. Importantly, this pluralistic approach to sources of evidence entails a risk-based evaluation of AI impacts on the SDGs. Some impacts are relatively certain and short term, while others are less certain and should be treated as such. Together, this provides the only workable foundation for anyone seeking to evaluate the future impact of AI on sustainable development in order to understand, develop, or regulate AI.

This book is intended for anyone with a desire to understand the potential, both positive and negative, of modern technologies to help shape our future. An interest in AI and sustainability will also be beneficial, and hopefully those who primarily know the SDGs will know a bit more about AI and vice versa. The purpose is to enable the reader to grasp the basics of the relationship between AI and the SDGs, and accessibility has been prioritized over in-depth technological or scientific expositions.

STRUCTURE OF THIS BOOK

In order to embark on the journey ahead of us without running the risk of getting lost, a road map is in order. Before any real analysis can begin, the key concepts must be established. The next chapter thus presents the SDGs and some of their background, before AI is defined and presented through certain examples related to the SDGs in Chapter 2. The next and final preparatory stage entails establishing the framework for analyzing the impacts of AI. In Chapter 3 I thus develop the framework that will be used throughout the rest of the book.

Next comes four chapters in which the impacts of AI are related to the economic (Chapter 4), social (Chapter 5), and environmental (Chapter 6) dimensions of sustainability before the overall impacts are considered in Chapter 7. There are 17 SDGs and 169 targets, and as this is an introductory book intended to give the reader an overall idea of how AI relates to the SDGs, this necessitates an approach in which certain goals and targets are analyzed in more detail than others. For some of the SDGs, the intention and content of the goal are relatively easy to deduce from its name. Some of the others are, however, so complex that they require a brief examination of the targets in order to make sense of the intentions behind them. The complexity of the goals is one determinant of the amount of space devoted to it, whereas the other one is the likelihood that AI impacts the goals significantly. How this evaluation is arrived at is the topic of the next chapter.

2

AI AND THE SDGs IN CONTEXT

In order to examine the potential of artificial intelligence (AI) to contribute to the Sustainable Development Goals (SDGs), we must first establish both what these goals really entail and what we mean by AI. Sustainability and AI have received enormous amounts of attention, and both concepts are used in a wide variety of ways. For the sake of clarity in the ensuing analysis of AI impact on the SDGs, a brief discussion of what is meant by sustainability, some context for the SDGs, and an explanation of what will count as AI is in order.

SUSTAINABILITY AND THE SDGs

The beginning of the modern concept of *sustainable development* serves as a useful origin story for the SDGs. In 1987, Gro Harlem Brundtland served as the chair for a UN commission that published the report *Our Common Future* (Brundtland et al., 1987). In that report, they defined sustainable development as:

> the ability to make development sustainable to ensure that it meets the needs of the present without compromising the ability of future generations to meet their own needs.

DOI: 10.1201/9781003193180-2

Key to such an understanding of sustainability is the acknowledgment of certain limits. These relate not only to the availability of resources and the environment's ability to absorb the effects of human activity, but also to the technological, social, and political limits. Sustainability is not only a matter of the state of the natural world, as our effects on the natural world are predicated by our social and political organization, and also our economic activity and technological development. In the report, they state clearly that in order to achieve sustainable development, three vital dimensions that must be emphasized simultaneously are as follows: the environmental, the social, and the economic dimensions (Brundtland et al., 1987). These will be referred to as the three dimensions of sustainability, and they demonstrate why AI is of interest with regard to sustainability. First, AI might change the technological factors that determine how effectively we use natural resources and our ability to monitor and keep track of these resources. Second, it might enable and promote innovation and economic growth, and this has implications for what sort of resources we use and how we use them, and also for how societies are organized, and the differences between societies.

Anyway, 1987 is a long time ago, and it might seem strange that goals related to sustainability are only now garnering attention. If that were the case, it would certainly be strange, but it is not. The direct predecessors of the SDGs were the Millennium Development Goals (MDGs). The MDGs consisted of eight goals, established in 2000 with an intended working period of 15 years (Sachs, 2012). Come 2015, and the SDGs were established, also with an intended 15-year working period.

The MDGs were, however, relatively limited in scope, and during the MDG period scientific evidence, popular opinion, and the political situation have changed, and this has prepared the ground for a more ambitious and broad set of goals to replace them. The SDGs were presented by the United Nations (2015), in the document *Transforming our world: The 2030 agenda for sustainable development*. The framework consists of 17 top-level goals, which are shown in Figure 2.1:

SUSTAINABLE DEVELOPMENT G⊙ALS

Figure 2.1 The sustainable development goals (United Nations, 2015).

These goals will be referred to as SDGs 1–17. The goals are based on the three dimensions of sustainable development. In addition to this, the United Nations uses five Ps to highlight the different areas of action: *people, planet, prosperity, peace,* and *partnership* (United Nations, 2015).

In addition to the top-level goals, each goal has a number of *targets* or subgoals. This means that goals such as the rather vague and ambitious SDG 13, "Take urgent action to combat climate change," has been operationalized and divided into more concrete targets that clarify what this urgent action entails, and the targets thus provide both the detail and direction required for making the goals actionable. For example, SDG 13 consists of the following targets:

13.1: Strengthen resilience and adaptive capacity to climate-related hazards and natural disasters in all countries

13.2: Integrate climate change measures into national policies, strategies, and planning

13.3: Improve education, awareness-raising, and human and institutional capacity on climate change mitigation, adaption, impact reduction, and early warning (United Nations, 2015).

In addition, there are often additional targets related to funding and practical aspects of reaching the goal. For SDG 13 we have 13.a regarding funding for action in developing countries and 13.b regarding capacity building in the most exposed and least developed countries (United Nations, 2015).

SDG 5 is another example, and while its title "Achieve gender equality and empower all women and girls" is seemingly simple, targets 5.1–5.6 and 5.a–5.c elaborate on the content and details of the SDG. The overarching goal is to "End all forms of discrimination against all women and girls everywhere," and other issues, such as violence, trafficking, forced marriages, equality in the home and in the workplace, sexual and reproductive health are detailed. In addition, the targets mention reforms, the use of enabling technologies, and policy and legislation. On an even more operational level, we find indicators for each goal, and these are quantitative measures that are proposed as guides on how to measure progress on the SDGs.

As this book is a relatively brief introduction to how AI relates to the SDGs, I will not be able to go into detail on how AI relates to all the different targets, as mentioned in the introductory chapter. I will also not explore the details related to the indicators for each SDG. However, the targets are sometimes crucial for understanding the context and intention of the goals, and when this is the case, the targets will be discussed to the extent necessary. As will become clear in Chapter 3, which details the analytical approach adopted in this book, the quantitative indicators are in and of themselves also considered to be relatively insignificant, as an analysis of AI impacts also requires that such measures are complemented by theoretical and qualitative methods of inquiry.

The SDGs are arguably extremely ambitious, and they cover a wide range of topics (Pekmezovic, 2019). This could lead to the objection that the framework and overall agenda are riddled by a lack of realism and specificity that might hurt the potential of realizing the goals. However, the SDGs are what is called *stretch goals* (Gabriel & Gauri, 2019), and such goals are not necessarily set only to determine a realistic target for our sustainability efforts, but also to provide us with a vision and stimulus for pursuing and daring to imagine both radical and ground-breaking solutions to the challenges we face. The realism of the goals themselves will not be discussed at length in this book, and the focus of attention will be on whether AI enables or prevents progress on each of the goals and the overall agenda. Rather than a shortcoming, the relatively vague and ambitious nature of the SDGs could in fact be considered a benefit, as the goals represent the aspirations of a united world community, and the level of ambition ensures that they will most certainly remain relevant until at least 2030.

One fundamental challenge for working with sustainability and the SDGs is that trade-offs will inevitably have to be made. The very concept of sustainability suggests that trade-offs between the short term and the long term are necessary. However, other trade-offs abound, such as the trade-off between economic growth and environmental protection, and for example how innovation and growth in free markets at times exacerbate instead of reducing inequalities, while it could be conducive to mitigating environmental challenges. Particular attention has been paid to the disconnect between the desire to combat climate change and reaching the rest of the goals. Combatting climate change (SDG 13) could, for example, undermine 12 other SDGs (Nerini et al., 2019). This points to the interlinkages between the various goals, such as economic growth (SDG 8) and the elimination of poverty (SDG 1). These interlinkages are crucial for understanding any effort to reach the SDGs as a whole (Le Blanc, 2015; Nilsson, Griggs, & Visbeck, 2016), and the concept of interlinkages is also key to the analytical approach adopted in this book, as described in the next chapter.

As should be clear from a quick glance and the SDGs, it is also easy to relate these to the concept of human rights. Such a linkage is also explicitly made by the United Nations (2015). However, as we will return to it in Chapter 7, while there is certainly overlap, there are also areas in which the two frameworks serve decidedly different purposes. In order to examine the social and human impacts more generally, and not only in relation to the SDGs, I'll show that frameworks such as human rights are also vital complements to the SDGs.

The question of the status of our current efforts to reach the SDGs will not be a question answered by me. As mentioned, the SDGs are stretch goals, and they will thus almost by their very nature remain relevant for the foreseeable future, and until the expiration of the SDGs in 2030. Interested readers will, however, find useful and updated information about the status of the SDGs through sources such as the sdg-tracker.org (Ritchie, Roser, Mispy, & Ortiz-Ospina, 2021), sdgindex.org (Sustainable Development Solutions Network, 2021), and various reports from both official and unofficial sources, ranging from reports on national progress to global progress on all or particular issues. In terms of environmental sustainability, the efforts of the International Panel on Climate Change (IPCC) are crucial for understanding both the need for and effectiveness of our efforts to combat climate change. As I am writing this book, the IPCC's working group 1 released the first IPCC report for some years, as they review and systematize the science related to the physical basis of climate change (IPCC, 2021). Their report constitutes a dire warning for mankind and thoroughly demonstrates that the efforts to reach SDG 13 cannot in any way be characterized as being on track.

ARTIFICIAL INTELLIGENCE

The next concept of importance for getting off the ground with this book is AI. The book is, after all, named after the technology which is found and referred to just about everywhere in modern society. Companies advertise how AI helps consumers solve their daily challenges more efficiently. Other companies sell AI systems to companies, and few would dare to be the only ones to openly state that they get along just fine without AI of any kind. Even governments use AI in a wide range of sectors, and through different types of applications (de Sousa, de Melo, Bermejo, Farias, & Gomes, 2019). The crucial question, then, is: what is AI?

While it could be interesting to go into the technical details on what AI really is, its history, and its various manifestations, I adopt a more general and practical approach to AI in this book. The overarching question we seek answers to is how AI can enable or prevent the reaching of the SDGs? and in order to start answering this question, the analyses must be based on a relatively broad working definition of AI. The important point is not to, for example, distinguish supervised from unsupervised learning, or to go into detail on the benefits of deep artificial neural networks. Rather, the point is to highlight what counts as AI and what does not, so that we do not confuse AI with digital technology in general, robotics, blockchain, and so on.

In order to get us there, I start with the definition used by Vinuesa et al. (2020), who consider AI to be:

> … any software technology with at least one of the following capabilities: perception—including audio, visual, textual, and tactile (e.g., face recognition), decision-making (e.g., medical diagnosis systems), prediction (e.g., weather forecast), automatic knowledge extraction and pattern recognition from data (e.g., discovery of fake news circles in social media), interactive communication (e.g., social robots or chat bots), and logical reasoning (e.g., theory development from premises). This view encompasses a large variety of subfields, including machine learning.

This means that most digital technologies can be considered *AI-based*. However, a solution or system will only be considered AI in this book if it depends significantly on AI in order to have sustainability-related impact. Digital banks and microfinancing, for example, might do wonders in terms of making financing, loans, etc. more easily available, and thus reducing inequalities. However, such technologies must be distinguished from AI "proper" in that digital technology and the use of computers, in general, is not necessarily AI. Digitalization, in general, will consequently not be discussed in this book. The same goes for, for example, robotics and automation. An industrial robot made to assist in the lifting of heavy equipment need not be

AI-based, but social robots used in, for example, healthcare and therapeutic interventions are clearly dependent on AI.

In brief, then, AI systems are computer-based systems in which the ability to sense and respond to their environments on a somewhat autonomous basis is key to its performing intended functions. These include apps, computer software for personal and industrial computers, robotic systems, many internet of things appliances, etc., and they are used both in the public and private sectors.

Examples of AI systems will be discussed in more detail in Chapters 4–6, which detail the various impacts of AI systems on economic, social, and environmental sustainability. Before that, however, we 'll have a look at some of what has already been said and done regarding AI and sustainability.

AI AND THE SDGs

As we have seen, sustainability is nothing new. Neither is AI, if we consider its historical roots in the early days of computer science (Bishop, 2006; Russell, & Norvig, 2014). Both AI and sustainability have, however, gained a lot of momentum in the last decades. Sustainability because of the increasing and overwhelming amount of scientific and everyday experience that highlight the changes we humans are responsible for causing. AI because of the vast increase in data availability and computing power – two aspects that leverage old methods and make them more powerful, accessible, and useful.

As the concepts in isolation have gained ground, we have recently also seen an increased interest in the combination of AI and sustainability, something that is also clearly visible from the fact that this very book has made it into your hands. However, also in academic journals new grounds have been prepared, and both old and relevant paths have been rethreaded. A slight detour to examine just what sort of other work has been done is in order before the main analysis commences. Both because it is important to know what has been done and thus needs no repeating, but also because it is the basis of much of the analysis that follows in the later chapters.

While much of the work done is what I consider partial and can most correctly be labeled *isolationist* analyses of technology (Barley, 2020), the various contributions are valuable as parts and input into a more complete and comprehensive analysis. What an isolationist approach is, and what sort of alternative is developed here, is the topic of the next chapter.

One of the more recent and influential accounts of how AI can contribute to the SDGs is found in Vinuesa et al. (2020). Their article in *Nature Communications* is brief, but is based on a rather detailed analysis of how AI might potentially relate to all the SDG targets, followed by a review of existing evidence of impact. They conclude that AI can enable the accomplishment of 134 of the SDG targets, while it can inhibit 59 targets. However, following the apparently positive conclusion is the disclaimer acknowledging that important aspects of AI are overlooked in much current research and that regulators need insight into the nature and potential of AI in order to respond properly to the proliferation of AI systems (Vinuesa et al., 2020).

While the article does not sufficiently account for the potential long-term, indirect, and unquantifiable effects of AI, their appendix with references to the works they have reviewed is highly valuable as a source for anyone wanting to perform their own analyses. Furthermore, their methodological approach and their perspective on the philosophy of science and what constitutes valuable knowledge is rather constrictive. However, even those that agree with them should find that the current book provides what is arguably an important addition to their work as it develops a framework for making sense of the overall impacts and how the various goals and targets are interrelated. Another attempt to identify the various impacts of AI on the SDGs is found in Chui et al. (2018). This work precedes the one just mentioned, and is arguably both more comprehensive and more balanced, and thus serves as another key source of insight for those wanting to pursue these issues further. A more recent account of how AI impacts the SDGs, based on preliminary versions of the framework developed in more detail in this book, is found in Sætra (2021a,c). A similar account that sees AI as part of a sociotechnical system, and calls for the need to examine both the sustainability of AI and the use of AI for sustainability, is provided by van Wynsberghe (2021), who mainly does this without basing the analysis on the SDGs.

Others have considered issues closely related to this book and the previously mentioned studies, but with a narrower focus on particular issues. Some focus on SDG 12 and sustainable business models (Di Vaio, Palladino, Hassan, & Escobar, 2020), others on the SDGs and the more technical aspects of AI (Khakurel, Penzenstadler, Porras, Knutas, & Zhang, 2018).

If we turn toward AI and sustainability more generally, and not the SDGs, there is a far broader set of research available, which also extends further back in time. Some examples are Toniolo, Masiero, Massaro, and Bagnoli (2020) and Yigitcanlar and Cugurullo (2020). While much research is not directly aimed at the SDGs, work on general sustainability, and ethical frameworks such as AI4People (Floridi et al., 2018) and work on responsible AI (Dignum, 2019), are often directly relevant to the analysis of the various SDGs.

This only serves to show a tiny slice of the available research relevant for examining the impacts of AI. Worth noting is the highly interdisciplinary nature of research on AI and sustainability. As the three dimensions of sustainability indicate, and the fact that we are focusing on the technology of AI, researchers from computer science and engineering, the social sciences, life and the natural sciences, and humanities, etc. must all eventually contribute to a full and proper understanding of how AI impacts our societies, our economies, and our environment.

SUSTAINABILITY AND AI ETHICS

3

THE CHALLENGE OF EVALUATING AI IMPACT

In order to evaluate artificial intelligence (AI) impact, what counts as impact must be clarified, and so must the method of analysis. In this chapter, I present the analytical approach and framework that will be used throughout the rest of this book. The analytical approach is built on two previous articles I have published on the subject (Sætra, 2021a, c), but while these preliminary articles in short-form have stopped short of demonstrating the potential of the framework in action, this book provides an opportunity to do just that.

First, I'll present the linkage between artificial intelligence (AI) ethics and the project undertaken in this book. Second, I move on to establish the analytical approach that allows for comprehensive and systemic analysis of AI and the Sustainable Development Goals (SDGs). This includes establishing the layered approach to impacts on the micro, meso, and macro levels, the separation of direct and indirect effects, and the acknowledgment that the various impacts cannot simply be counted, but that their consequences must be evaluated in terms of degree. Finally, I'll present a framework for presenting the results arrived at with such a method, as developed from the work done in Sætra (2021c).

DOI: 10.1201/9781003193180-3

SUSTAINABILITY AND AI ETHICS

Any analysis of the impacts of AI is by necessity connected to the discipline of AI ethics, which is, as the name implies, concerned with the analysis of the ethical implications of AI (Coeckelbergh, 2020; Müller, 2020). Sustainability is, after all, intrinsically based on deeply ethical questions related to whether we owe anything to future generations, what constitutes a just distribution of resources, the problems of discrimination and various forms of inequality, the value of nature, etc. AI ethics provides a broad foundation of research that points toward sustainability-related impacts, and thus provides a fertile ground for examining how AI impacts the SDGs.

Some of the issues that have garnered much attention from the AI ethics community are related to issues of how AI is used in surveillance and how it impacts privacy (Sætra, 2019a, 2020b; Solove, 2000), and also how a lack of privacy and the increased availability of personal data allow for AI-based manipulation and persuasion (Sætra, 2019c; Yeung, 2017). Furthermore, a key focus area is the nature of bias in AI systems (Buolamwini & Gebru, 2018; Müller, 2020; Noble, 2018), as I'll repeatedly return to in the coming chapters. One fundamental notion related to the ethics of AI is that technology – AI included – relates to the distribution and exertion of power (Culpepper & Thelen, 2020; Gillespie, 2010; Sagers, 2019; Sattarov, 2019), and distributional issues are key to understanding the SDGs. Furthermore, others have examined how AI, for example, as used in social robotics, changes human relationships (Turkle, 2017). Not just interpersonal relationships between few people, however, as AI is also enmeshed in the debates regarding increased polarization due to the dynamics of social media, the use of AI in the dissemination of fake news, the creations of deep fakes, etc. (Sætra, 2019b; Sunstein, 2018).

As I consider AI to be part of larger sociotechnical systems, as I'll shortly return to, the issues related to the nature of data, and in particular access to, ownership, and use of it, is central for understanding some of the most important sustainability-related impacts of AI.

Data is not, and can never be, neutral (Sætra, 2018). In addition to this, data is at the very core of what is referred to as *surveillance capitalism* (Zuboff, 2019), which is an important concept in the analysis of the current economic and political systems.

ANALYTICAL APPROACH

This book presents a new framework for systematizing the analysis of the ethical impacts of AI by examining the impacts through the three main dimensions, 17 goals, and, when necessary, their associated targets. By doing so, we are able to see how AI affects the economy, social phenomena, and the environment, and from these broad categories, we can delve deeper and deeper into a nuanced understanding of AI impacts. The SDGs thus represent a new framework for AI ethics that allows for more effective interdisciplinary discussions about AI ethics, as well as more effective public communication and the generation of awareness regarding the impacts of AI. The SDGs cover a wide range of issues, but we'll do well to remember that there are certain issues that remain unexplored by the SDGs, which I'll discuss in Chapter 7.

I've called the SDGs an effective tool for ethical analysis, but how exactly do 17 goals help us perform the ethical analysis? Answering this requires me to more fully develop the framework that is used in this book, as we must be able to distinguish different forms of direct from indirect AI effects, and it is also beneficial to distinguish between three different levels of analysis: the micro, meso, and macro.

DIFFERENT FORMS OF DIRECT AND INDIRECT EFFECTS

Throughout this book, I'll refer to direct effects and indirect effects. This is an important distinction, as AI will in some instances be used in ways that directly impact the SDGs, individuals, and organizations, but it is also characterized by a range of impacts that are indirect. These indirect effects might be related to how AI can, for example, engender economic growth (SDG 8), which will in turn potentially have major effects on efforts to combat poverty (SDG 1). The difference between how an impact on one goal leads to impacts on other goals and direct impacts are what I will usually refer to when I distinguish between direct and indirect effects. This is shown in Figure 3.1.

There are, however, also other forms of indirect effects, and the effects just discussed will thus often be referred to as *ripple effects*, as they are characterized by the spread of impacts from original direct impact areas.

As we find ourselves in the domain of sustainability, the notion of *scopes* of impacts is also relevant for illustrating how AI impacts can be more or less direct. The Greenhouse Gas Protocol (GHG Protocol) is a framework for analyzing and categorizing emissions, and in this framework, one distinguishes between scope 1, 2, and 3 emissions (World Resources Institute, 2021). The exact details of the GHG Protocol are of less interest here than the idea of scopes of impact.

A reformulation of the GHG Protocol that captures AI-based sustainability-related impacts will, first of all, be based on a particular company or organization. It is thus useful for considering how one

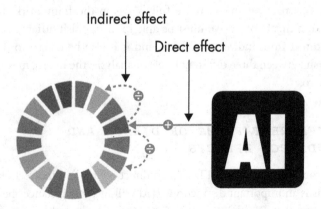

Figure 3.1 Direct and indirect effects.

actor's actions have effects, but also how these actions have effects both upstream and downstream. Scope 1 impacts are the direct impacts caused by the company's own development and application of AI systems. This might, for example, entail considerations of how an IT company is able to use AI to optimize the energy efficiency of their client's building, which contributes to reduced energy use and reduced emissions, but also how their internal computing infrastructure generates emissions through power use, the generation of waste, etc. Scope 2 impacts, however, entail considerations regarding the power and electricity, heat, and cooling used to provide those solutions. The company might use an external data center in the provision of their own services, and while the emissions resulting from the data center are in a sense external to the company, they are directly related to the company's activities, and must thus be considered an indirect impact from the company. While the company does not produce the emissions themselves, the emissions would not exist without the company's activities. In this example, increased use of power and the associated emissions must consequently be considered against the positive contributions captured by scope 1. Scope 3 impacts might involve all other indirect impacts caused by the company's activities – both upstream and downstream. The purchase of computing equipment that relates to SDG 12 and sustainable consumption and production, for example, might be considered here. A key aspect to include in scope 3 impact assessments will, however, also be how any AI system developed and sold is used by others and the sustainability-related impacts of such usage. Does a company's system help others to, for example, downsize and automate tasks? Is it used for employee surveillance? Does it lead to risks of AI-based discrimination, etc. Scope 3 impacts can of course also be positive, in that the indirect use of the company's solutions can be used to improve infrastructure, monitor, and safeguard worker's rights, etc. (Figure 3.2).

A SYSTEMIC AND LAYERED APPROACH

The notion of scopes and impacts external to the actor in question reveals that I have adopted a systemic approach to AI as a technology.

Figure 3.2 AI impacts and scopes 1, 2, and 3.

AI is not an isolated technology, and its application will always be characterized by impacts beyond its direct context. Seeing AI as part of a larger sociotechnical system means that AI as a technology will be assumed to have impacts on the political and economic systems, while these systems will also be assumed to constrain and guide the evolution of both the development and use of AI. To understand the impacts of any technology, including AI, its role in and relation to the sociotechnical system must be considered (Barley, 2020). Doing the opposite entails performing what Barley (2020) refers to as *isolationist* analyses of technology. While such analyses might be of some importance, as they provide case studies and use cases that can be considered input to a more comprehensive analysis (Vinuesa et al., 2020), how AI is used in isolated experiments and closed systems will here be considered to be of little importance in and of itself. The broader system I refer to is as mentioned today at times referred to as "surveillance capitalism" or a "data economy" (Véliz, 2020; Zuboff, 2019). Others prefer to focus on the role of platforms and consequently refer to platform capitalism (Gillespie, 2010; Mills, 2020; Sagers, 2019). Another key debate revolves around the question of whether AI is an integral part of industry 4.0 and the fourth industrial revolution (Schwab, 2017), or if such accounts of the impacts of AI and smart technologies are manifestations of hype and insufficient attention to the real nature of technological change (Barley, 2020). I will refer to these phenomena at times, but for a full account of the details of the sociotechnical system, the reader will have to refer to more comprehensive accounts. Of some importance, however, is the notion of Big Tech, as I will refer to this term throughout this book. It usually refers to the largest technology companies, and Google, Amazon, Facebook, Apple, and sometimes Microsoft, are usually considered to be the main corporations encompassed by the term (Foer, 2017; Herrman, 2019; Sen, 2017). These are all American companies – a fact that is of special importance with regard to the SDGs' focus on local and equal access to technology. Other companies, and countries are, however, also major players in the world of AI, and China, in particular, is home to several of the main challengers to the US-based Big Tech companies, such as Alibaba and Tencent.

Since AI is assumed to have such effects on larger systems, a final source of indirect sustainability-related impacts emerges. If AI contributes to changes in the distribution of power between, for example, private companies and the government, this will in turn have a wide range of potential effects on the various SDGs, as these power shifts manifest themselves in the change of the sociotechnical system. Figure 3.3 shows the complete representation of the analytical framework.

The final part of this framework is the distinction between impacts on the micro, meso, and macro levels. AI might, for example, be used to create systems that allow individuals to improve their health and nutrition, and such impacts on individuals and small groups are considered micro-level effects. Meso-level effects, however, relate to how AI impacts groups of more significant size, and in this book, it

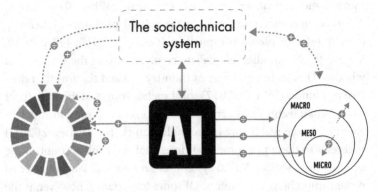

Figure 3.3 The analytical framework.

involves considerations of how large organizations, classes, nations, and even regions, are impacted by AI, with a particular emphasis on differential impact, as this is crucial for understanding the aims and goals of the SDGs. The macro level is the level of political, economic, and production systems, and long-term impacts of AI on our economies and societies in the broadest sense (Jonsson, 2016). The macro-level effect is where considerations related to politics and the sociotechnical systems belong and this is also the level at which analyses of the nature and potential for, for example, industrial revolutions occur (Barley, 2020). Moving from the micro level to the macro level, we also tend to move from short-term to long-term considerations of impacts (Jonsson, 2016), and the interplay between the different levels is discussed in more detail in Chapter 7.

The complete analytical framework is outlined in Figure 3.3, which shows how AI impacts the SDGs directly, but also indirectly through ripple effects and through its impacts on the sociotechnical system. In addition, it shows how AI has differential impacts on the micro, meso, and macro levels, and that impacts from one level to another are also of importance.

I have presented what might seem like a wildly ambitious framework thus far in this chapter, and I completely understand the reader who has by now started to wonder how all this can be put to use.

Such concerns are quite natural, and I for now want to emphasize that this framework is mainly intended to highlight and force considerations of the wide range of indirect sustainability-related impacts AI has. I have no intention to use it to provide a final answer that summarizes all the impacts of AI, but rather to provide the reader with the necessary scope to know where we have to look in order to find all important impacts. A too ambitious framework will by necessity entail that we cannot go deep into all the detail and nuances. However, I consider this far less of a downside than the alternative. Choosing a framework simple enough to allow all its detail to be considered in an introductory book about AI and the 17 SDGs is, I argue, far too simple to provide a realistic and useful account of the true impact of AI.

A FRAMEWORK FOR SYSTEMATIZING AI IMPACTS ON THE SDGs

Based on the analytical approach just described, I have developed a framework for presenting the results of an analysis based on the approach. I have previously examined how this framework could be used for the purpose of evaluating and reporting on sustainability-related efforts for companies (Sætra, 2021c), and there I presented a preliminary version of the framework that is more fully developed in this book. For those interested in using this book for the preparation of sustainability reporting, I recommend referring to that article for more detail.

The main feature of the framework for summarizing and presenting the results of the analysis is the production of tables such as the one presented in Figure 3.4. In the chapters that follow, you will see that the key questions related to how AI impacts each SDG on the micro, meso, and macro levels are presented, along with an overview of which of the other SDGs the SDG in question ripples to and from. The left side of the table summarizes the positive impacts, while the negative impacts are summarized on the right side.

Figure 3.4   Summary of AI impacts on a single SDG (Sætra, 2021c).

4

SUSTAINABLE ECONOMIC DEVELOPMENT

One of the most often-discussed ways in which artificial intelligence (AI) is argued to impact the Sustainable Development Goals (SDGs) is through its effects on the economy. AI, proponents will argue, enables various beneficial innovations and scientific advances, and it can make existing modes of economic activity more effective. This, one might conclude, would clearly indicate that AI has a significant potential positive impact on the economy-related SDGs.

The goals detailed in this chapter are the following:

SDG 8 (decent work and economic growth)
SDG 9 (industry, innovation, and infrastructure)
SDG 10 (reduced inequalities)
SDG 12 (responsible consumption and production)
SDG 17 (partnerships for the goals)

However, I'll argue that the popularized accounts regarding the positive sustainability potential of AI are somewhat one-sided – or exaggerated – due to a lack of according for the actual content and nuances of the goals related to, for example, economic growth and innovation.

While it might seem strange to deal with SDG 17 under the banner of economic sustainability at first, this is partly a side effect of the

DOI: 10.1201/9781003193180-4

fact that the three dimensions of sustainability arguably underplay the importance of the political domain. However, the three dimensions are so established that breaking this convention makes little sense in a book such as this, and it suffices to say here, and in the concluding chapters, that politics is vitally important for reaching all and any of the SDGs. While SDG 16 (which is categorized as a social goal) and SDG 17 go some way towards describing the kinds of political activity required to enable the reaching of the SDGs, they still leave much of the political territory underexplored.

SDG 8

Promote sustained, inclusive and sustainable economic growth, full and productive employment and decent work for all (United Nations, 2015).

Right off the bat, it seems clear that both "decent work" and "economic growth" are momentous goals that in and of themselves could have been the focus of entire frameworks of goals. I share such an impression, and will consequently split both these goals and SDG 9 into the main components covered by the goals. This is necessary in order to meaningfully explore how AI impacts these goals, as AI might, for example, impact economic growth positively while simultaneously creating fundamental challenges related to the decency of work. SDG 8 will thus be split into 8a, which will refer to economic growth, and 8b, which refers to the decency of work.[1]

SDG 8A – ECONOMIC GROWTH

As already touched upon, AI has had a huge impact on the world of business. The fact that just about all sectors and industries these days either have already implemented or are examining how to implement big data and AI systems, in order to stake out their positions in both the current and the future world of business, points to the fact that AI is more than just hype. AI has indeed been a catalyst for technological change, economic growth, and the creation of value, and this entails that AI impacts on the economic SDGs are significant.

A key point to remember when dealing with economic growth is that it can be considered something of a foundational goal. Economic growth might, after all, allow us to solve problems related to the scarcity of resources, and thus eliminate poverty, fight starvation, allocate more resources to saving the environment, etc. However, this is premised on the assumption that economic growth in and of itself is a good thing. Trickle-down economics, and the notion that a rising tide will lift all boats, has been a staple of many varieties of growth fetishism, but modern history has not always been too kind to these theories. While economic growth has been achieved in times of liberal politics and economics, this has led to a situation of increased inequality, both globally and in the US (Piketty, 2014). As clearly stated in SDG 8, the kind of growth imagined is *sustained, inclusive, and sustainable*. This necessitates going much deeper into the nature of economic growth, while growth for growth's sake is of little interest.

Big Tech is the term often used to refer to the largest American technology companies that constitute the acronym GAFAM – Google, Amazon, Facebook, Apple, and Microsoft (Petit, 2020). Whatever one desires to call the economic system that has grown forth through, or alongside, their growth – the data economy, platform economy, surveillance capitalism, etc. – the fact is that a select few companies have become immensely valuable and today command a substantial portion of global capital. All these companies are key players in the development and deployment of AI, and their role in the creation of economic growth is thus relevant to examining the broader impacts of AI on the goal of economic growth. In short, Big Tech has been at the head of a growth that does not seem particularly conducive to achieving the kind of economic growth described in SDG 8. While there has been growth, the growth seems to have increased, rather than diminished, inequalities.

The richest people, in the richest countries, are now richer than ever and control an unprecedented share of total wealth (Chancel, 2019). Accurate and indisputable depictions of inequality are hard to come by, but few question the fact that inequality is a challenge for modern societies, as also clearly indicated by SDG 10, which entails a particular focus on this. Chancel (2019) provides an account of current inequalities, and his research indicates that both between-country and in-country inequality are high and increasing. While inequality has traditionally often been discussed as the problematic difference between rich and poor countries – and rich and poor regions – in-country inequality is increasingly important, and instead of nationality, class is seen to be the key factor to describe current inequalities globally (Chancel, 2019).

Sustained, inclusive, and sustainable economic growth says something fundamental about the kind of growth we desire. Just as we would not like an uncontrolled cancerous growth in our bodies, but rather a controlled and purposive growth compatible with health and longevity, we need to see how AI might contribute to this. I argue that identifying whether AI enables SDG 8a requires us to look at the interplay between SDGs 8 and SDG 10 in particular (reduced inequalities), but also on the social and environmental goals, as positive impacts on these will have indirect effects on SDG 8 and will allow us to see what kind of growth AI promotes. This means that the final verdict on AI impacts on SDG 8a partly depends on the analyses that follow, and that it can be more fully examined in the later chapters discussing the overall impacts on the goals as seen in relation to each other.

However, the positive potential of AI in terms of promoting economic growth is indeed important, as growth is considered essential for reaching any of the goals. The SDGs and agenda 2030 are not premised on the notion of, for example, degrowth (Latouche, 2009), but on the idea that the right kind of growth will allow us to create a sustainable future. AI is clearly associated with the potential for such growth, and the main purpose of the preceding considerations has been to highlight how recognizing this is only a first and preliminary step that must be followed by an analysis of the nature of this growth.

AI is a force that can both inhibit and enable the achievement of SDG 8a. Understanding the nature of the growth engendered by AI, and the causes that determine how AI influences growth the way it does is consequently a key area for future research. Furthermore, it is an important focus area for politicians and others who aim to promote sustainable AI-based growth, as they must make sure that AI research and development is conducted in ways conducive to sustainable growth, but also that the results of such research and development are disseminated and deployed in ways that ensure the same.

With regard to direct effects on SDG 8a, AI has been shown to promote growth, but it is highly uncertain whether this growth can be characterized as sustained, inclusive, and sustainable. More precisely, deeper analyses will find examples of how AI can and does contribute to such growth, but that it simultaneously is a factor promoting the opposite. For example, there is little evidence to support the notion that AI enables the targets of inclusive growth and at least 7% gross domestic product (GDP) growth per year in developing countries. Much of the growth created by AI is generated in rich countries – and captured by Big Tech. Some also speak of the spread of the AI-enabled data-based economy as a form of new colonialism, as tech-startups in the developing world tend to be bought and controlled by western owners (Müller, 2016; Truby, 2020).

The indirect effects of AI-enabled economic growth are both numerous and important, and these will mainly be mentioned in the context of the goals in question. It suffices to state here that these effects will also be both negative and positive, as economic growth might, for example, promote health and education, but it could also increase inequality, increase consumption, and in turn lead to negative environmental impacts. The key in any analysis of AI and economic growth will be to adopt a broad enough perspective to ensure that the nature and the distribution of growth are factored in.

SDG 8B – DECENT WORK

The other part of SDG 8, which relates to decent work, is also clearly impacted by AI. The direct effects are potentially large, both because of how AI changes jobs and the tasks people perform at work, but also because of how AI is used to control and monitor workers, and also how AI-based automation changes the very structure and distribution of work.

First of all, if AI helps us achieve sustained, inclusive, and sustainable economic growth, this will lead to the creation of new jobs and new opportunities for decent work. On the flipside, non-inclusive economic growth based on, for example, AI automation generated by proprietary systems owned and controlled by large companies might hurt both the prospects and decency of work.

As jobs are automated, some might indeed be relieved of tedious work that humans arguably never should have performed in the first place (Danaher, 2019; Pistono, 2012). However, whether or not this is a good thing depends entirely on the alternatives available for those who lose their jobs. The focus of SDG 8b is the creation of decent work opportunities for all, and not some utopia in which machines perform all the work while humans are free to pursue other interests. In lieu of institutions and systems that will guarantee that those worst off will not be made even worse off through the automation of work, AI-based automation poses a threat to the achievement of SDG 8b. Solutions such as universal basic income and extensive welfare states are potential ways of facing increased automation (Bregman, 2017), but it is not the solution described by SDG 8b. The preceding considerations relate to the potential macro-level effects of AI on the structure of work, unemployment, taxation, and regulation.

Second, AI also impacts individuals. AI can be used to assist workers in physically and mentally taxing jobs, and thus improve their situations. AI-based systems, such as robots, can also help perform tasks that are dangerous and performed in hazardous environments. Some workers might also enjoy AI-based systems that help them plan and improve their work. However, AI is also increasingly used in surveillance and in the implementation of manipulative practices at the workplace. As all forms of work become increasingly digital, employers get more data for analysis, and this can be used both to monitor, but also to influence, workers (Anderson, 2017).

Third, the preceding consideration indicates how AI can impact work on the meso level through changes in the power relations

Positive Impacts Does AI...	SDG 8	Negative Impacts Does AI...
• Improve working conditions? • Strengthen individual autonomy?	+ Micro -	• Change work and tasks for the worse through automation? • Reduce the decency of work? • Contribute to increased workplace surveillance and a reduction of autonomy and liberty, etc.?
• Lead to productivity growth for relatively disadvantaged groups or local and regional businesses, etc. • Increase the power of marginalized workers?	+ Meso -	• Engender increased differences between groups?
• Lead to sustained growth? • Improve people's life quality? • Improve the situation of the least well off?	+ Macro -	• Lead to non-inclusive growth? • Lead to a kind of economic growth not in line with the requirements listed in the targets of SDG 8? • Lead to sustained growth, or is AI partly based on hype and non-lasting growth? • Contribute to unemployment through automation?
All goals are potentially positively affected by a positive contribution to 8	+ Ripples to - + Ripples from -	All goals are potentially negatively affected by a negative contribution to 8 13, 14, 15

between employers and employees, and through, for example, promoting temporary or gig-based work which changes the power of unions, etc.

SDG 9

> Build resilient infrastructure, promote inclusive and sustainable industrialization and foster innovation (United Nations, 2015).

SDG 9 is also a compound goal that AI potentially impacts heavily, and I have therefore split it into SDG 9a (innovation), 9b (infrastructure), and 9c (industry). These three phenomena are clearly related, but while it might make sense to group them together in one goal, it also makes sense to disentangle them for analytical purposes.

SDG 9A - INNOVATION

Of the eight targets under SDG 9, the following two relate most close to innovation:

- 9.5: Enhance scientific research, upgrade the technological capabilities of industrial sectors in all countries, in particular developing countries, including, by 2030, encouraging innovation and substantially increasing the number of research and development workers per 1 million people and public and private research and development spending.
- 9.b: Support domestic technology development, research, and innovation in developing countries, including by ensuring a conducive policy environment for, inter alia, industrial diversification, and value addition to commodities.

One of the most heralded benefits of AI is its use in research and innovation, both in the public and private sectors. However, when one examines the targets of SDG 9, we clearly see that the SDGs are not mainly concerned with innovation in itself, but with a particular form of innovation related to domestic technology development and access to information and communication technology (ICT). This also shows why a superficial reading of the SDGs, including briefly noticing the focus on economic growth and innovation, might lead people astray if they do not proceed to examine the actual content of the goals.

If we consider AI to be a hypothetical technology isolated from any linkages to sociotechnical systems, access to data and infrastructure in the form of computing power, and ownership and exclusivity, it is clear that AI has great potential to foster innovation. However, cutting-edge AI systems are developed in a relatively limited set of countries (Zhang et al., 2021), and even if these systems might conceivably be applied equally in any country or region, SDG 9 focuses on domestic development and the development of domestic technological capabilities. Without this emphasis on local development and ownership, the benefits of AI innovation might indeed lead to benefits locally, while profits, capabilities, and competencies are extracted to the nations in which the key companies operate. AI-based innovation is highly dependent on data, and this means that securing competitive local AI development also requires a change in the structures related to data gathering and sharing. This could happen through an increased gathering of domestic data, sharing of data gathered in developed countries, or the limitation on the storage and use of data already gathered and used by existing companies.

The reason we need to focus on data in order to democratize AI is that the generation of and access to historically unprecedented datasets is what has driven recent progress in AI (Marcus & Davis, 2019). AI innovation requires both infrastructure – which will be discussed shortly – and access to data in order to secure universal, fair, and equal access to the benefits of AI. However, even without this, we might see AI systems forming the basis of new scientific discoveries and innovations that will potentially positively influence all people, and SDGs, in the long run.

While equality and access to technology are important, one might here, as with economic growth, also test the argument that innovation and research are subject to cascades of benefits – or trickle-down innovation. Even if some people get the benefits first, some might argue, this will lead to a situation in which these benefits gradually become available to all. While this might be problematic for SDGs such as number 10 which concerns inequality, it might indeed lead to benefits related to, for example, SDG 3 and good health and well-being.

Scientific progress and innovation are susceptible to AI impacts, but even more important is how the ripple effects from AI-related impacts on SDG 9 on all other goals is arguably the most important contribution of AI. Throughout this book, I argue that a large proportion of the positive and negative AI impact on other SDGs are in fact due to the impact on SDG 9. As mentioned in the previous chapter, this relates to the distinction between direct and indirect effects, and means that if we are not to count the same thing twice, foundational progress on SDG 9 caused by AI should primarily be counted here, and not as separate impacts on all the 16 other goals. However, the indirect effects are important and will be discussed in the following analyses, often with an acknowledgment that some of the impacts are ripple effects from SDG 9. One important consequence of this approach is that by not counting impacts twice, we get a better basis for examining the overall impact of AI on the SDGs in Chapter 7. SDG 9 will be considered a keystone goal for reaching all the other SDGs, and it will thus often be mentioned in the table showing which goals lead to indirect positive and negative impacts on the other ones.

Another key feature of the book is the focus on the double-edged nature of AI. While innovation and scientific advances are crucial for achieving sustainability, this is no reason to disregard the fact that innovation and science can be just as much a force for unsustainability in the wrong hands as they can be a force for sustainability in ideal situations. As noted by Arthur Koestler (1967), an invention cannot be uninvented. Even if technologies such as the atomic bomb have arguably not been a force for good, they are, he states, here to stay. Not just weapons, but all technologies "can serve the powers of light or of darkness" (Koestler, 1967, p. 377). Although written over 50 years ago, these insights remain pertinent in today's context, as the question of AI systems combined with weapon and military technology is an increasingly controversial topic. An age-old prophecy from dystopic science fiction movies is made real as autonomous weapon systems and "killer robots" now exist (Sparrow, 2007), thanks in large part to AI.

We must keep in mind that the same technologies – such as AI-enabled drones – can, as we will see, be used to deliver aid or bombs, to destroy a country's infrastructure, or to survey and protect vulnerable land areas or species. Innovation and scientific progress are important, but the progress we achieve can never be entirely neutral, and it must thus continually be evaluated based on (a) the goals of our societies and (b) the applications of the technology (Næss, 1989). In this book, the SDGs are taken as our societies' goals, and while innovation is key for reaching them, the wrong kind of innovation might also undermine their reaching them. As local development and capacity building is key for reaching the goals, the fact that much current AI innovation occurs in the US and China, and largely in private companies, is a major challenge for unleashing the hypothetical positive potential of AI. Rapid innovation in these companies can both exacerbate inequalities between groups, countries, and regions, and it is also important to note that private sector innovation and research is not subject to the same ethical guidelines and principles as those that apply to academia.

SDG 9B – INFRASTRUCTURE

Moving on to infrastructure, we see that four of the eight targets of SDG 9 are clearly related to this topic:

- 9.1: Develop quality, reliable, sustainable, and resilient infrastructure, including regional and transborder infrastructure, to support economic development and human well-being, with a focus on affordable and equitable access for all

- 9.4: By 2030, upgrade infrastructure and retrofit industries to make them sustainable, with increased resource-use efficiency and greater adoption of clean and environmentally sound technologies and industrial processes, with all countries taking action in accordance with their respective capabilities
- 9.a: Facilitate sustainable and resilient infrastructure development in developing countries through enhanced financial, technological, and technical support to African countries, least developed countries, landlocked developing countries, and small island developing States
- 9.c: Significantly increase access to information and communications technology and strive to provide universal and affordable access to the Internet in least developed countries by 2020.

Once again, we see that the kind of infrastructure improvement detailed is aimed at improving the situation of developing countries and reducing existing inequalities. The targets focus on regional and transborder infrastructure, which means that SDG 17 – partnerships – will be tightly related to reaching this goal, and they also specify that the infrastructure should be of high quality, reliable, sustainable, and resilient.

Another fact that makes connecting the analysis of AI impacts to sociotechnical systems crucial, is how the targets require affordable and equitable access for *all*. This highlights the need to see beyond isolated use-cases and experiments, and to examine the very structure in which AI is developed, applied, and in which it can be useful. Target 9.a explicitly calls for developed countries to provide enhanced financial, technological, and technical support to developing countries. While energy, water, roads, etc., are clearly part of what is referred to as infrastructure, ICT is explicitly mentioned, as increased access to ICT and universal and affordable access to the internet in developing countries is a target of its own. This is crucial for the analysis of AI impacts, as a well-developed ICT infrastructure is crucial for achieving the kind of local and domestic development of AI systems as discussed with regard to innovation. I have already mentioned the importance of data, and in addition to the required competency to build AI solutions, a proper computing infrastructure with the necessary computing power and connectivity is required.

Does AI, then, contribute to affordable and equitable access to infrastructure? Access to data and computing infrastructure is, as of now, arguably not what can be referred to as universal, affordable, and equitable, and this challenge is made worse by the fact that AI-related technology – the innovation and development just examined – is often proprietary and conducted in and by private corporations. This means that even if the infrastructure was available, this alone is no guarantee that developing countries would be able to make use of AI in ways that reduced inequalities and promoted local development. Infrastructure is thus intrinsically linked to the economic and political systems that relate to the distribution and control of intellectual property.

Proponents of AI are quick to point out how AI can be used to make infrastructure more efficient, to create new solutions, "smart grids," and even smart cities (Serrano, 2018). This is indeed a potential benefit of AI, but it also highlights another problematic aspect of AI. As AI becomes more tightly integrated with infrastructure, the questions of control and ownership of the solutions used become increasingly important. In parts of the world, AI has become enmeshed in the technologies that constitute our everyday environments, both at home and at work. Both public and private sector organizations now rely on such systems, it forms the basis of the smart cities built around the world, and AI is increasingly being built into all sorts of digital solutions (Engström & Strimling, 2020). Even those that do not really require or directly benefit from AI get it, and while part of the explanation is that AI helps sell products, another is that AI can be used to analyze and generate highly valuable data about all types of users. In short, AI has, in a certain sense, become infrastructure, and in a sociotechnical system so heavily dependent on technology, the large technology corporations have amassed power. Private companies might indeed ensure that the technology they control is available universally, affordably, and equitably, but if they do not do so, the domain of politics will have to intervene if AI and associated technologies are to become an enabler for the SDGs (Sætra & Fosch-Villaronga, 2021).

On a less ominous note: the potential positive impact of AI on infrastructure will not be overlooked in what follows. As AI has the potential to help make the development or utilization of infrastructure more efficient, it has the potential to promote better access to infrastructure. If AI solutions are open and accessible, and developing countries take the responsibilities given to them by target 9.a seriously, AI can indeed be part of the solution that will improve infrastructure in the developing world. If this is done by providing developing countries with the best solutions available, it might even help reduce inequalities and provide the foundation for a future in which further progress on all the SDGs based on domestic development can be imagined.

SDG 9C – INDUSTRY

The last part of SDG 9 is industry, and three of the targets relate specifically to this (9.4, which was also placed under infrastructure, relates both to infrastructure and to industry):

- 9.2: Promote inclusive and sustainable industrialization and, by 2030, significantly raise industry's share of employment and GDP, in line with national circumstances, and double its share in least developed countries
- 9.3: Increase the access of small-scale industrial and other enterprises, in particular in developing countries, to financial services, including affordable credit, and their integration into value chains and markets
- 9.4: By 2030, upgrade infrastructure and retrofit industries to make them sustainable, with increased resource-use efficiency and greater adoption of clean and environmentally sound technologies and industrial processes, with all countries taking action in accordance with their respective capabilities

Industry and AI are clearly linked, and much work on AI related to making the industry more effective, for example, through automation and robotization. Once again, we see that the targets specify a particular form of industrialization, and the notions of sustainable and inclusive industrialization are here highlighted. It is also worth noting that the targets specify goals related to increasing both the size and the role of industry in developing countries. This might seem controversial, as increased industrialization might seem to be inimical to reaching the environmental goals. However, since the targets specify that the growing industry should be sustainable, this would partially alleviate this concern. Nevertheless, the promotion of economic growth and industrialization by the SDGs is a cause for concern for those concerned with reaching the environmental goals. This is where proponents of *green growth* and *de-growth* face-off, but this is a topic too large to be covered in this book, and the possibility of green growth will be accepted since the framework for analysis is the SDGs which is based on such a view. The targets do mention the possibility of small-scale industry, and the role of financing and the need for basing such industrial growth on the sustainable innovation and infrastructure just examined are emphasized. Industry for a sustainable future, then, is what AI must promote, and this is an industry that is both people friendly and environment friendly.

As infrastructure and innovation form the basis of progress on SDG 9c (industry), the basis of AI impact on this part of SDG 9 has partially been covered already. The most important ways in which AI can enable this goal are through sustainable innovation and automation. However, the question of automation is a tricky one, particularly as the industry in question is required to be inclusive. In a highly innovative and sustainable industry based on automation, novel solutions related to the ownership of the means of production, or the dissemination of wealth generated from these means, must be examined if such a development is not to increase differences and be exclusionary. The impact of industry on the other SDGs is potentially high, and the important question is whether AI today is in fact a force for people and environment friendly industrialization – a form of industrialization that benefits the least developed countries the most.

Positive Impacts Does AI...	SDG 9	Negative Impacts Does AI...
• Help researchers and innovators?	+ Micro -	• Increase dependency on expensive and exclusive technology?
• Increase availability of infrastructure?	+ Meso -	• Strengthen the relative position of developed countries and groups?
• Improve the potential for small-scale and sustainable industry?		• Engender increased use of proprietary and private technology in public infrastructure?
• Promote transborder and regional infrastructure?		
• Promote local innovation, industry, and quality infrastructure.	+ Macro -	• Promote exclusive and proprietary technology and infrastructure?
		• Promote industrial growth at the expense of environmental goals?
		• Contribute to the creation of autonomous weapons?
8 in particular, and potentially all other goals through innovation.	+ Ripples to -	8, 10, 13, 14, 15
4, 17	+ Ripples from -	

SDG 10

Reduce inequality within and among countries (United Nations, 2015).

The reduction of inequality is intimately linked to achieving inclusive economic growth, innovation, infrastructure development, etc., and the main AI-related impact on SDG 10 will thus come about as ripple effects on these and other goals. The 10 targets for SDG 10 naturally emphasize improving the situation of those least well off, and details goals for income growth, empowerment and inclusion, regulation of financial markets, enhanced representation in decision-making.

All this is to be achieved by the principle of special and differential treatment of developing countries, with a particular emphasis on the least developed countries. Target 10.2 shows that inequality is not only – or even primarily – related to wealth, as social, economic, and political inclusion is the goal. Furthermore, target 10.3 cuts off certain lines of arguments in favor of liberal technology policy as it states that not only equality of opportunity matters, but also equality of outcomes.

Saying that AI will have direct effects on SDG 10 would imply arguing that AI can be used to redistribute means, or that the use of AI disproportionately favors those least well off. Both of these arguments seem strenuous, and will not be pursued further here. As we have already covered, there are in fact big obstacles to overcome if AI is to become force for reduced inequalities, and many of the effects already discussed would indicate that AI has a negative impact on SDG 10. On the macro level, AI can contribute to increased differences as the key technology companies command ever-larger shares of the global economy (Chancel, 2019; Petit, 2020). On the meso level, we see the differences between groups increasing (Chancel,

Positive impacts Does AI ...	SDG 10	Negative impacts Does AI ...
• Empower the least well off? • Promote inclusion? • Raise income?	+ Micro -	• Give advantaged individuals even larger advantages?
• Provide disproportionately large positive benefits to the developing countries and marginalized groups?	+ Meso -	• Give advantaged groups and nations even larger advantages?
• Provide ways to improve the situation of the least well off?	+ Macro -	• Lead to increased concentration of wealth and benefits and exacerbate existing differences?
1, 2, 3, 4 8, 13, 14, 15, 17	+ Ripples to - + Ripples from -	8 8, 16

2019), as we will also pursue further in the examination of SDG 1 (the elimination of poverty) in the next chapter. On the micro level, we might also see increased inequalities following the growth of AI, as those with access to and control of AI-based systems used in, for example, automation, will increase their power and capacity to extract resources to the detriment of those without similar means.

SDG 12

Ensure sustainable consumption and production patterns (United Nations, 2015).

Sustainability is at its core a quite simple concept, as it states that what we use cannot exceed what is replenished. Earth Overshoot Day[2] marks the date each year in which we have used more resources than what is regenerated – in which the earth's biocapacity is exceeded by humankind's ecological footprint – and it is largely used to show that this occurs quite early each year. In 2021 it was July 29, which implies, vastly simplified, that the remaining 5 months of the year is marked by excess use of the earth's resources. In order to improve this situation, both consumption patterns and production patterns must be changed.

SDG 12 clearly shows that sustainability can only be achieved by making changes happen on the macro, meso, and micro levels, and that none of these alone will suffice. The targets call for a 10-year framework of programs, in which developing countries must take the lead. It goes on to detail what sort of consumption and production is targeted. This is improved management of natural resources, a halvation of food waste, management of chemicals of waste through life cycles in order to reduce the release into the environment, and reduced waste in general through prevention, reduction, recycling, and reuse.

Furthermore, it calls for encouragements for companies, "especially large and transnational companies," to adopt sustainable practices and to report properly on their sustainability impacts, to increase the active use of public procurement power, and to ensure that all individuals have the required information to consume sustainably. This is all to be achieved through the support of developing countries, through the development and implementation of tools to monitor sustainability impacts and to rationalize inefficient fossil-fuel subsidies.

AI impacts on this goal will partly by indirect, for example, through the innovation and industry aspects of SDG 9. However, AI can also be used actively in the monitoring of sustainability impacts, and while SDG 12 refers specifically to the importance of tourism, monitoring systems for sustainable consumption and production, in general, is clearly relevant for the intention of this goal. In combination with new and improved sources of data, AI can be used to monitor passively or even to proactively intervene in order to encourage sustainable consumption and production practices.

This impact of AI hits the micro, meso, and macro level, as monitoring is required not only for policymakers, but also for companies and individuals. Having an app that tells a person the carbon impact of their choices, the products they use, the electricity and water used at home, etc., could conceivably have an important educational effect. Add to this the ability of such AI systems to optimize usage, and we'll have a potential positive impact of AI on SDG 12. This is also one aspect of AI that might not be as susceptible to the double-edged nature of AI, as I'll assume that quite few will have the incentives to *increase* their ecological footprint when they get more and better information. The creation and active use of incentives will be crucial for achieving sustainable consumption and production. Unless policy-makers reward the desired patterns of consumption and production, and disincentivizes the opposite, the AI systems in question might be used to maximize cost savings or profit through unsustainable patterns instead of contributing to the reaching of this goal.

On a more negative note, the question of whether AI drives responsible consumption must be answered by also considering the sustainability of the proliferation of products connected to the internet-of-things and the potentially shorter life cycles of complex and technologically advanced products that replace conventional products. A television set, for example, which previously got its content from a central source, is now a computer of its own, and many consumers will have experienced how even relatively new smart-TVs will alert them that certain apps will no longer be updated for their TVs, and that they have to purchase a new one. In a world where all appliances are increasingly computers of their own – even washing machines, dishwashers, refrigerators, etc., the possibility of higher product turnover and the effective implementation of planned obsolescence, is a challenge for SDG 12, and AI is increasingly often the key selling point when the need to upgrade is promoted.

Positive Impacts Does AI …	SDG 12	Negative Impacts Does AI …
• Help individuals monitor their consumption? • Help individuals understand the sustainability of the products and services they use?	+ Micro -	• Lead to increased consumption?
• Help companies and other organizations produce and consume more sustainably?	+ Meso -	• Help companies or others to more effectively implement, for example, planned obsolescence or drive consumption in other ways?
• Reduce the use of natural resources and the generation of waste through increased monitoring and optimization of processes?	+ Macro -	• Increase consumption without a proportionally larger reduction in the negative impacts of consumption?
13, 14, 15 9, 17	+ Ripples to - + Ripples from -	8, 9 8, 9

The major benefit of AI on SDG 12 might thus be the optimization of material used in production, and also innovation related to new materials, and not least circular economic practices. However, AI improved production need not mean that AI must be a part of the products made. Furthermore, AI provides educational opportunities and monitoring capabilities that potentially provide a significant positive impact.

The positive effects of AI on sustainable consumption are thus potentially both positive and negative, and it is imperative that macro-level policies are implemented in order to ensure that the incentives for actors on the meso level – the businesses – are in line with the goals of sustainable development. Without proper policies, the incentives of the producers and users of AI in products and production might lead to increasingly unsustainable production patterns and efforts to make consumption patterns even more unsustainable than they are today.

SDG 17

Strengthen the means of implementation and revitalize the Global Partnership for Sustainable Development (United Nations, 2015).

The final economic SDG is perhaps the one in which AI cannot be argued to have a particularly big impact. AI might play a role in monitoring systems for compliance, for example, in which case it might be said to improve both the chances of partnerships being formed and the chances of any partnership being successful. This is, however, more related to the creation and implementation of effective monitoring systems in general, and not necessarily dependent on AI to a significant degree.

My reason for arguing that AI has a minor impact is seen more clearly if the targets of SDG 17 are considered. They relate to, for example, domestic mobilization of resources for sustainable development, mobilization of resources (finance) in general, follow-through by developed countries on their development assistance, coordination of policies. Of particular importance are the need to assist least developed countries, to enhance science sharing and cooperation across regional and North–South (and South–South) boundaries, and crucially:

> Promote the development, transfer, dissemination and diffusion of environmentally sound technologies to developing countries on favourable terms, including on concessional and preferential terms, as mutually agreed (Target 17.7).

The latter target strikes at the core of the problematic nature of AI as a tool for sustainable development. As heavily emphasized throughout this book, AI has great potential, but unless the distributional aspects related to AI are figured out and addressed, AI will superficially enable the reaching of slogans seemingly similar to the SDGs, while actually undermining the reaching of the goals as properly understood by examining the intention of the goals and the targets that make up the goals.

Positive Impacts Does AI …	SDG 17	Negative Impacts Does AI …
• Promote inclusion? • Help generate and spread knowledge?	+ Micro -	
• Enable preferential treatment of developing countries?	+ Meso -	• Disproportionately favor the advantaged?
• Provide improved means for partnerships through AI-based monitoring and transparency?	+ Macro -	
All, and 13, 14, and 15 in particular.	+ Ripples to -	10
1, 9, 10, 16	+ Ripples from -	8, 9

AI will thus be the subject matter and a key topic when partnerships and sought and formed, and when policy and regulation are developed and harmonized globally. AI and the associated technologies and infrastructure are one of the key focus areas for technology transfer and diffusion is the SDGs are to be reached. This will not occur through the use of AI globally by a small number of powerful companies in selected countries. AI will have a positive impact only when AI capacity is built domestically, with a particular focus on the least developed countries, and where access to AI – including the development, tailoring, and deployment of them – is both fair and equitable.

The sociotechnical system in which Big Tech currently holds a key position can thus be argued to be a key inhibitor of SDG 17, while AI as a hypothetical technology holds great promise if the current obstacles to its fair and equitable use are removed. This can, however, only happen through the active and resource-demanding efforts of developed countries, and this is, when it all comes down to it, what SDG 17 is all about.

NOTES

1   My use of 8a, 8b, etc., for discussing the various aspects of SDGs 8 and 9 must not be confused with the *targets*, which contain periods, and is referred to as 8.a, 8.b, etc.

2   https://www.overshootday.org, accessed date 31 July 2021

5

SUSTAINABLE SOCIAL DEVELOPMENT

While the term sustainability tends to lead the mind toward forests and climate gas emissions, *people* are heavily emphasized in the Sustainable Development Goals (SDGs). Nine goals are categorized as social goals, and they relate to a broad set of issues:

- SDG 1 (no poverty)
- SDG 2 (zero hunger)
- SDG 3 (good health and well-being)
- SDG 4 (quality education)
- SDG 5 (gender equality)
- SDG 6 (clean water and sanitation)
- SDG 7 (affordable and clean energy)
- SDG 11 (sustainable cities and communities)
- SDG 16 (peace, justice, and strong institutions)

Poverty, hunger, health, and education are the first four goals that aim directly at improving the situations of the worst off, and gender equality is the fifth. In addition to this, there are slightly more technologically oriented goals related to clean water and sanitation (6) and clean energy (7), while the latter two in this group detail requirements for sustainable communities and institutions (11 and 16).

DOI: 10.1201/9781003193180-5

SDG 1

End poverty in all its forms everywhere (United Nations, 2015).

The first SDG is perhaps also the most ambitious. In fact, it is difficult to imagine a more ambitious goal than to end all poverty, in all forms, everywhere. How then, might artificial intelligence (AI) contribute to ending poverty? First of all, I consider the indirect effect of promoting inclusive growth (SDG 8) the main potential positive impact of AI on the elimination of poverty. While some have argued that AI has the potential to positively impact all targets of SDG 1 (Vinuesa et al., 2020), we must consider how this might come about, and not least whether such impacts are directly related to SDG 1 or mainly the indirect effect of enabling the other goals. Furthermore, as SDG 8 is as a key goal for reaching SDG 1, it is worth remembering that economic growth in itself need not necessarily contribute to reduced inequality and a reduction of poverty, as discussed in the previous chapter.

If we assume that AI has great potential to influence SDG 1 through economic growth, the key question is asking how AI might contribute to the kind of growth that would eliminate poverty. First of all, we must distinguish between economic growth and its effects on the reduction of poverty and another goal, namely the reduction of inequalities (SDG 10). Significant economic growth could potentially lead to a situation in which inequalities increase while the number of people living in absolute poverty is simultaneously reduced. The tide might indeed raise all boats, even if some boats are raised far higher than others are. This requires us to distinguish between absolute and relative poverty. The first is concerned with how many people live below certain resource thresholds, while the latter relates to how little those with the least have relative to those with the most. The AI-powered locomotives of the current economy – Big Tech – might promote economic growth, which reduces absolute poverty while it also exacerbates existing inequalities and increases relative poverty. The targets also refer to technology and equal access to economic resources, including "appropriate new technology ...

Positive Impacts Does AI ...	SDG 1	Negative Impacts Does AI ...
• Raise individuals from national poverty levels?	+ Micro -	• Contribute to increased relative poverty?
• Enable solutions that improve the situation of the poor and vulnerable?	+ Meso -	• Contribute to the relative disadvantage of particular groups?
• Lead to economic growth, allowing for poverty reduction?	+ Macro -	• Lead to economic growth of a kind that mainly provides benefits to those already well off?
2, 3, 10 8, 10, 17	+ Ripples to - + Ripples from - 8	

including microfinance" (United Nations, 2015), and while AI might be a part of technological solutions aimed at the poor and the vulnerable, these technologies could also increase differences unless technology transfer and the assistance from developed countries is secured through reaching SDG 17.

Consequently, when people argue that AI has a positive effect on *all* the targets related to poverty, this relies on an isolationist account of AI and technological change, and arguably a lack of accounting for the broader concept of relative poverty and the broader effects of AI-induced economic growth.

SDG 2

End hunger, achieve food security and improved nutrition and promote sustainable agriculture (United Nations, 2015).

Moving on to the goal of ending hunger and improving nutrition, we see that the positive potential of AI is much greater. New technologies, related both to innovation and research related to genetically modified crops, etc., but also to the use of AI in agriculture in order to increase efficiency, could arguably lead to both new sources of food, improved nutrition, and increased access to food.

Agriculture has been industrialized and mechanized, and smarter automation can be seen as a continuation of this trend, in which AI plays an important role. Examples of AI used in self-driving farm equipment and robots and AI combined with sensor data in order to make irrigation and fertilization, etc., demonstrate how AI can make agriculture both more resource-effective and more effective in general.

The potential inhibitors related to AI and the food system are that these solutions are relatively costlier to implement than traditional agriculture, and there is thus a risk that such solutions will mainly be used by those who already have access to both food and resources in general. Such a development could negatively influence, for example, SDG 10 (increased inequalities). Furthermore, the emergence of genetically modified crops, etc. could promote economic growth and agricultural efficiency (Huang, Pray, & Rozelle, 2002). However, it also promotes a development in which natural resources are turned into proprietary products in which both seeds and produce are largely controlled by large corporations, which will in addition have control over the means to effectively fight pests, etc. (Raney, 2006).

For AI to contribute positively to the elimination of poverty and improved nutrition, the solutions in question must be available for those with the least resources, and this requires, for example, open-source solutions and the sharing of insights derived from AI, and the sharing of and perhaps even subsidization of technologies from the rich to those with more meager means.

The automation of agriculture is a clear instance of technological change that can be labeled infrastructural, as traditional modes of production are made untenable by new technologies (Barley, 2020). An example of how seemingly small technological leaps impact a range of social factors is found in Pelto's example of the introduction of the snowmobile in Skolt Lapland. This led to broad and deep changes in the distribution of both wealth and work, and also in social relations (Pelto, 1987).

A final potential negative impact of AI is seen in how innovation and research in food and agriculture cannot be assumed to lead to more nutritious and accessible food for all. Instead, one might argue that those in control of the most sophisticated AI systems will use these to develop the most profitable crops, and these can easily be imagined to be the ones that taste the best and most effectively boosts demand. The emergence of corn as the staple agricultural product of parts of the US serves as a warning of how research and development need not lead to societally beneficial effects (Parker, Salas, & Nwosu, 2010).

Furthermore, as AI-driven agriculture can be assumed to be more effective, there is reason to fear that its impact on the environment will be even larger than today's agriculture, and thus not what one might call sustainable. Parts of the world are already producing an excess amount of food, but instead of distributing these excesses to those in need, it is destroyed, as those who own this produce have few incentives to unbalance and undermine their own markets in

Positive Impacts Does AI …	SDG 2	Negative Impacts Does AI …
• Improve the supply of healthy food? • Help individuals understand their nutritional needs?	+ Micro -	• Increase the need to use costl95y systems and proprietary agricultural solutions? • Enable the creation and more effective marketing of unhealthy foods?
• Allow for the effective use of new land areas enabled by new crops, etc?	+ Meso -	• Worsen the situation for small-scale farmers? • Change the balance between workers and landowners, and between agricultural regions/actors?
• Drive agricultural innovation and effectivity gains?	+ Macro -	• Engender a more exclusive and proprietary food system?
3 1, 8, 9, 10, 17	+ Ripples to - + Ripples from -	3, 8, 10

such ways. There are few reasons, other than naïveté, to assume that AI changes this. For AI to have positive effects on the alleviation of hunger and improved nutrition, this will have to be coupled with political and economic mechanisms to promote the potential enabling effects of AI while preventing the inhibiting effects.

SDG 3

Ensure healthy lives and promote well-being for all at all ages (United Nations, 2015).

The next SDG is related to the previous, as nutrition is clearly linked to healthy living, and as a consequence – well-being. Health is a crucial component of sustainability, as it is perhaps the most important determinator of the sustenance of individual lives. It impacts the welfare, economics, and politics of a society drastically, and it is also clearly impacted by environmental factors. Based on previous accounts of AI impact on the SDGs, which state that AI positively impacts 69% of the targets, while only negatively impacting 8% of them (Vinuesa et al., 2020), this could be a cause for great optimism. However, how does AI impact health and well-being?

Once more, the positive ripple effects from SDG 9 – innovation – are an important part of the picture. Health innovation and research contribute to the combatting of diseases and causes of unhealth, while other forms of welfare technology increase well-being for those with various challenges related to mental and physical health. One example of the latter could be how social robots are used to provide care and social interaction for the elderly with dementia, while AI is also used to find a cure for and to diagnose the affliction itself (Sætra, 2020a). In addition to this, AI is increasingly being used in therapeutical situations, and it arguably provides a resource-effective and therapeutically effective way to improve mental health without the need for human therapists (D'Alfonso et al., 2017). As we'll see in relation to the use of AI in educational settings, such developments might improve both access to and the quality of therapy.

Such innovations relate directly to the macro-level healthcare infrastructure, but AI is also highly implicated in micro-level health and individual's lives. A wide range of apps and technologies are today used to track individual's health, activity, and nutrition, for example. One example is health-tracking functionality built into smartphones, while the increasingly ubiquitous fitness and health trackers of various kinds track just about all aspects of individual's lives. Their activity is one thing, but these devices do more as they track sleep patterns, menstrual cycles, heart rates, etc., all with the promise of both keeping track of and identifying worrying patterns. In addition, apps can analyze and help plan individual's meals and diets, and all in all, one might argue that such AI-based apps are important in fostering healthy living.

It is thus easy to see how AI might be argued to enable the reaching of SDG 3. However, while there is certainly a positive potential in AI, this does not mean that there is not simultaneously a negative potential. The recurring theme in this book is just the double-edged nature of AI, and this applies here as well. First, some have pointed out that self-tracking and the quantification of the self is not necessarily a good thing (Lupton, 2016, 2019). Second, it is difficult to argue that the emergence of AI, Big Tech, and social media, has been accompanied by a general improvement in the mental (or physical) health of those who use AI-based technologies the most. On the contrary, AI-based social media is at times associated with increases in mental unhealth and general declines in well-being. While there are indications of such negative potential of AI, the evidence is as of yet inconclusive (Appel, Marker, & Gnambs, 2020).

Finally, while both societies and individuals might see health and welfare-related benefits from AI, the technologies and solutions in question are costly. Health differences are already associated with differences in class, and while the decadent upper class may at one point in history have been associated with both obesity and unhealthy lifestyles, the opposite is the case in modern western societies (Young et al., 2018). If expensive AI-enabled fitness equipment, training regimes, and nutrition plans are indeed effective, this

Positive Impacts Does AI …	SDG 3	Negative Impacts Does AI …
• Enable people to track and improve their physical and mental health?	+ Micro -	• Lead to negative psychological effects?
• Make advances in health technology and science available to new groups?	+ Meso -	• Promote health for the advantaged and increase inequalities?
• Provide societies with new insight and solutions to more effectively combat disease and afflictions in order to promote public health?	+ Macro -	• Lead to scientific breakthroughs and new solutions that are mainly available to developed nations rather than decreasing inequality?
8, 9 1, 2, 9, 17	+ Ripples to - 10 + Ripples from - 8	

development can be assumed to further increase such inequalities. As improved health is positively associated with most aspects that foster well-being and reduced inequalities, it is imperative that AI is used to reduce, and not increase differences between people and societies. One further aspect of these considerations relates to where and how AI is applied. Are the resources being used to tackle the afflictions that strike those best well off, or is it rather being used to solve the main challenges of the developing world?

SDG 4

Ensure inclusive and equitable quality education and promote lifelong learning opportunities for all (United Nations, 2015).

Education is one area in which technology has for a long time been hailed as the harbinger of progress. Computers are already integral parts of education in large parts of the world, and as new technologies and devices such as iPads, etc. have come along, their introduction in educational settings has not been far behind. While the use of computers and other screen-based devices are not intrinsically linked to AI, having access to screen-based devices in school is often a requisite for making use of the advances of AI, which I focus on in the following.

For educators and leaders in schools, AI has one primary use in the analysis and use of data about learners. In educational settings where computer systems are used, new data is often generated. This leads to new possibilities for analyzing data and using such analyses for improving education, not only at an aggregate level (school, school district, region, nation, etc.), but also on an individual or group level (individual learners, but also particular groups of learners, such as children with autism spectrum disorder). AI can help those in charge learn what works, and what does not, and education can purportedly be adapted and tailored in order to be more effective. This is the main benefit derived from *learning analytics*, and while regular statistics can produce a number of important benefits on the basis of such data, AI systems provide added benefits in terms of analysis and its use in education planning and tailoring of learning systems. However, the databases are often enormous, complicated, and can properly be categorized as *big data* of a kind that is often difficult both to maintain and make use of without the use of AI (Laney, 2001).

While AI can be used to support teachers in their work, AI is also increasingly being used *as* a form of teacher. One example is in the form of intelligent tutoring systems (ITS), which has proven to have some potential benefits, even if they are as of yet somewhat limited and do not constitute a full alternative to human teachers (Heaven, 2019; Nwana, 1990). Social robots are another technology, in which AI is instrumental, and such robots are used in a range of educational settings, and particular attention has been devoted to the use of such robots in intervention and training with children with autism spectrum disorder.

The preceding considerations highlight the potential for AI to improve the quality of education, but as the description of SDG 4 clearly shows, quality is not all, as this education must be inclusive and equitable, and also promote lifelong learning. While AI might improve quality, one potential negative impact relates to how the implementation and effective use of learning analytics, ITSs, social robots, etc. are costly and require a robust national educational infrastructure. Without that, AI increases the risk that education for those best off will be improved, while others will not benefit from this. If so, increased inequality is a potential result.

However, AI might also be used in ways that promote inclusive and equitable learning, and one particular opportunity is making ITS and AI-improved education available *remotely*. AI-based education might be exclusionary, but it could also give rise to a situation in which the very best quality of education is made available to most, or all. This will, however, require that proprietary solutions are made available to all, that open-source solutions and content is made available, or that governments and companies form partnerships through which technology and educational material are made available. This involves spreading quality education both to nations and to groups that do not have the resources to develop or purchase access to it themselves. It also entails improving access to education for groups that have traditionally been considered beyond the scope of fundamental education, as lifelong learning is increasingly important in a technologically advanced future where, for example, automation changes the nature and scope of work (Danaher, 2019).

Big Tech is today highly involved in the development of education technology (EdTech) systems, and in order to make AI an enabler of SDG 4, it is important to make sure that governments and the civil society are involved in, and have control over, the gathering and analysis of learning data and the educational infrastructure. The positive impact of AI on SDG 4 is potentially of great importance, as improved education in the developing world, particularly for groups that have previously not had access to it, would have major ripple effects on a number of other SDGs. Particularly SDG 5 (gender equality), SDG 10 (reduced inequality), SDG 8 (economic growth and decent work), SDG 9 (innovation, industry, and infrastructure), and SDG 16 (peace, justice, and strong institutions) are intimately linked to inclusive and equitable quality education.

Positive Impacts Does AI ...	SDG 4	Negative Impacts Does AI ...

• Improve the quality of
  education?
• Allow individuals to learn
  in new situations?
• Improve access to quality
  education for all?
	+ Micro -
	
	+ Meso -
		• Enable surveillance
		  and manipulative
		  practices in
		  educational settings?
		• Mainly improve
		  education for those
		  with access to costly
		  systems and those
		  who speak particular
		  languages, etc.?

• Improve knowledge
  generation on a societal
  level?
	+ Macro -	• Increase the digital
		  divide within and
		  between nations?

5, 8, 9, 16 9, 17	+ Ripples to - + Ripples from -	10

SDG 5

Achieve gender equality and empower all women and girls (United Nations, 2015).

Inclusivity and equality are central to the SDGs, but gender equality is one topic that is perceived as so important that it has gotten a goal of its own. While one might want to argue that equality related to ethnicity, LGBTQ status, etc. is equally important, SDG 5 clearly limits its focus to women and girls. Nevertheless, issues of AI impacts on discrimination and equality are relevant to SDG 5 *and* other issues, and I use this as an opening for a broader discussion of how AI enables or inhibits discrimination of various types.

One potential positive impact of AI is that a range of innovations related to work at home, and services or infrastructure that reduces the need for home work, might help emancipate women and girls from domestic work, and thus facilitate their entry into paid work in other sectors and increase the potential for autonomy and careers. Such effects might come about through the general ripple effects stemming from enabling SDG 8 and SDG 9. In addition, the ripple effects resulting from improved access to quality education (SDG 4) are also important for enabling SDG 5.

More generally, some might also argue that the use of AI in decision-making processes can enable us to overcome human biases, and thus combats discrimination related to work, financing, political processes, etc. However, while a computer might in a certain sense be perceived as objective in principle, it is never objective in actual applications. Through human involvement in the construction of AI systems, the choices related to what sorts of data is gathered, how the data is gathered, how the data being coded, etc., human biases are inevitably introduced also in AI systems (Sætra, 2018; Sayer, 1992). Furthermore, data is in many instances historical data based on human-driven processes, and when AI systems are made to learn from historical data, historical biases are introduced in such systems. While bias resulting from direct human involvement is a known challenge, the biases that are implemented through AI systems are often very hard to both understand, identify, and to rectify, due to the rather opaque nature of AI and the challenges related to making proper AI systems that are transparent and that can explain the decisions made to humans. A lot of important research has been produced on the numerous ways in which AI systems can negatively impact vulnerable or marginalized groups, including women and other minorities (Buolamwini & Gebru, 2018; Noble, 2018).

Target 5.b specifically mentions how enabling technologies can help empower women. This implies that AI might indeed have some positive potential, but it is important to be aware of the potential pitfalls just mentioned, and also the fact that AI is not necessarily a significant factor in most enabling technologies. In addition, much work remains to be done in making sure that enabling technologies are women-friendly, as a key challenge in the technology industry is that a large majority of developers are men (and white). This might lead to situations in which the technologies developed are particularly useful for those similar to the developers, and less useful, or positively harmful, for women and other groups underrepresented in the population of developers and producers.

Positive Impacts Does AI …	SDG 5	Negative Impacts Does AI …
• Empower women and girls? • Lessen the work load in the home? • Help combat discriminatory practices? • Enables a higher percentage of women to participate in the workforce?	+ Micro - + Meso - + Macro -	• Discriminate against individuals? • Discriminate against groups? • Engender a situation in which certain groups are not represented in the development and ownership of AI systems?
4, 8, 10 4, 8, 9	+ Ripples to - + Ripples from -	10 8, 9

SDG 6

Ensure availability and sustainable management of water and sanitation for all (United Nations, 2015).

Water and sanitation systems can be more effectively managed through AI systems, and SDGs 9a (innovation) and SDG 9b (infrastructure) could have a significant and positive impact on access to water and more effective management of water. AI-based water infrastructure is; however, costly, and for such solutions to become available to those most in need, and thus not lead to increased differences, international partnerships and technology transfer will be vital. This goal is also clearly related to SDG 14, which entails the conservation and sustainable use of oceans, seas, and marine resources. The relationship might, however, be both positive and negative. On the one hand, increasing people's access to water and sanitation might entail solutions that negatively impact non-human access to and use of various types of water. However, this goal states that *sustainable management* is a goal, and reaching this goal might thus also entail that improved and more sustainable management of water for people simultaneously improves environmental aspects.

Positive Impacts Does AI …	SDG 6	Negative Impacts Does AI …
• Provide individuals with easier access to water and sanitation?	+ Micro -	• Benefit those already well off the most?
• Provide new groups with access to clean water and sanitation?	+ Meso -	• Increase inequalities between groups with regards to access to clean water and sanitation?
• Improve public infrastructure and the quality of water and sanitation?	+ Macro -	• Make societies more vulnerable due to the increased technological infrastructure of water and sanitation systems?
3, 10, 14 9, 17	+ Ripples to - 10 + Ripples from - 8, 9	

The positive impacts of AI might be based on the development of new and innovative methods for purifying water, AI systems can be used to monitor water quality, and it can be used to optimize infrastructure and by reducing waste also improve access to water. Unless significant innovation engenders new methods for providing access to clean water, however, minor improvements in the efficiency of existing infrastructure could be argued to be of relatively limited importance.

Meanwhile, AI-based systems that increase access to water will, if proprietary, lead to increased differences. In addition, such systems could be more vulnerable to errors and hostile attacks, and thus require attention to both physical security and cybersecurity.

SDG 7

Ensure access to affordable, reliable, sustainable and modern energy for all (United Nations, 2015).

Access to affordable, reliable, sustainable, and modern energy for all is somewhat similar to the previous SDG, which detailed access to water and sanitation. Once, more, SDG 9, both in terms of innovation and infrastructure, will be vitally important for reaching SDG 7, and the key impacts of AI are thus assumed to be the indirect effects of reaching SDG 9.

The main benefits of AI would be related to more efficient systems of production, planning, and distribution of energy. In addition, AI might promote the development of new and more efficient sustainable energy sources, and could thus increase the amount of energy that qualifies as relevant to SDG 7. However, if innovation and improved infrastructure are to enable the reaching of SDG 7, the solutions in question must once again be made available to those most in need.

Another potential benefit of AI in relation to energy is the environmental benefits associated with renewable energy sources. However, SDG 7 mainly mentions *sustainable* energy, without thoroughly defining what sort of energy qualifies as sustainable. Depending on the energy sources, there will be different effects on SDG 13 (climate) and SDG 15 (life on land). SDG 14 (life in water) is also related to energy sources, as marine windmills proliferate.

Increased access to energy is important for a wide range of goals, as energy availability would cause positive ripple effects on SDG 8 and SDG 9, as both economic growth and industry, innovation, and infrastructure are vitally dependent on energy (Nilsson et al., 2016).

Positive Impacts Does AI …	SDG 7	Negative Impacts Does AI …
• Enable low-cost and innovative access to energy?	+ Micro -	• Make traditional forms of life untenable through modernization and electrification?
• Provide new groups with access to energy?	+ Meso -	• Improve access to and quality of energy for those who already have it?
• Promote energy-based economic growth and innovation?	+ Macro -	• Lead to significant increases in energy use and consumption?
1, 2, 3, 8, 9, 10, 13 9, 17	+ Ripples to - + Ripples from -	12, 13, 14, 15 8, 9

The negative implications of AI impacts on SDG 7 might be related to any general increase in the production of energy, rather than making the existing energy mix and infrastructure more sustainable and effective. Increased production of energy could lead to negative impacts on a range of goals, such as responsible consumption and environmental goals. This is particularly relevant if AI impacts on energy access and the type of energy used are not mainly aimed at those who need it the most.

SDG 11

Make cities and human settlements inclusive, safe, resilient and sustainable (United Nations, 2015).

Examining cities and human settlements entail a consideration of the social arrangements in which we all reside, and this is consequently a goal of enormous breadth and range. The goal is to make settlements inclusive, safe, resilient, and sustainable. Inclusivity is partly related to the goal of reduced inequality and gender differences, but it can also be interpreted far more broadly. Notions such as universal access and the accommodation of both physical and mental variation are potentially covered by the notion of inclusivity, and so is nationality, ethnicity, etc. Safety is another large topic, and this encompasses both phenomena such as crime and violence, but also natural disasters and environmental threats, as indicated by the mention of resilience. Lastly, the settlements are to be sustainable, which almost goes without saying as it is a sustainable development goal. However, this could be taken to mean that all human settlements must be conducive to economic, social, and environmental sustainability. The number of issues potentially impacted by AI seems also boundless, but we will here focus on some of the most important potential impacts, particularly related to the targets of SDG 11.

One key way in which AI promises to impact human settlements is through the development of *smart cities* – technology-intensive cities in which sensor data is analyzed and used to improve and optimize existing services, as well as preparing the grounds for new ones. The UN, for example, has launched an initiative for promoting sustainable and technology-intensive cities through knowledge transfer across the globe (International Telecommunication Union, 2020). AI can be implemented in a number of ways when technology is emphasized in city planning and development, but it is important to remember that not all things high tech and digital are necessarily AI. However, AI can serve important functions in optimizing existing solutions and infrastructure, and the indirect effects of positive impact on SDG 9 will thus be highly relevant for enabling SDG 11.

Sustainable settlements are, however, far more than science fiction-like cities in which everything is connected to sensors and computer systems. It is also about safety and inclusion, as we have seen. One way AI can improve security is through increased use of surveillance and analysis of data in order to both predict and solve crime. Predictive policing, for example, is one potentially effective, but also highly controversial, example (Shapiro, 2017).

One issue being emphasized by parts of the AI ethics community is the concern about what they call the "prison to tech pipeline," in which technology is used in potentially problematic ways. There have, for example, been calls for the abolition of facial recognition technology, as such technologies can perpetuate racism and camouflage and hide a range of biases (Coalition for Critical Technology, 2020).

However, while AI might arguably be used to analyze and mitigate human biases, and surveillance might, in theory, be used to identify problems of racism or exclusionary practices, there is little evidence as of yet to support the idea that AI significantly contributes to more inclusive human settlements. Some might say that if our experience with AI up to now is to be our guide for evaluating its impacts, its use by police – but also the enthusiastic adoption of such technologies by non-democratic and illiberal societies – highlight the clear risks AI poses to inclusivity and safety for all. Surveillance-based AI systems might be argued to foster safety in terms of fighting crime, but the SDGs are also built on the values of human rights and the notion that democratic values and liberty also matters.

Positive Impacts Does AI ...	SDG 11	Negative Impacts Does AI ...
• Increase individual's safety?	+ Micro -	• Reduce liberty and privacy through increased use of surveillance
• Allow for the inclusion of previously marginalized groups?	+ Meso -	• Favor the safety and resilience of particular well-off groups?
• Lead to safer and more resilient societies?	+ Macro -	• Promote non-democratic and authoritarian technosolutionism?
3, 6, 7, 10 9, 10, 13, 14, 15	+ Ripples to - + Ripples from -	10, 16 8

Safety is important, but not at all costs. Another potential negative impact of AI is how it might lead to increased polarization and conflict, which is also a potential threat to safe and inclusive settlements (Sætra, 2019b).

In terms of resilience, however, AI shows more positive potential. The ability to analyze data enables the more effective forecasting and identification of threats to settlements. This relates both to the threats and to weaknesses that arise in, for example, a settlement's infrastructure, and to the potential external threats posed by a changing climate and natural threats. Insight generated by AI systems might be used to respond more effectively in a time of crisis, but even more importantly, AI systems might also be used for planning and adapting to potential threats before they occur.

SDG 16

Promote peaceful and inclusive societies for sustainable development, provide access to justice for all and build effective, accountable and inclusive institutions at all levels (United Nations, 2015).

While politics is at times seemingly obscured in the SDGs, goal 16 clearly highlights the crucial role politics plays in achieving sustainable development. The focus is on peaceful and inclusive societies, justice, and effective accountable, and inclusive institutions – at all levels. SDG 16 is thus a compound and highly ambitious goal that might just as well have been split into several different goals.

First of all, one might ask: how can AI enable justice, inclusion, and sustainability in politics and societies? As we have already covered in the examination of SDG 11, AI can be used by police and government to secure order and prevent crime. This is one way in which AI can arguably also be conducive to the provision of justice. However, as discussed, such usage of AI is riddled with challenges related to a lack of transparency, oppression, and discrimination (Noble, 2018; Sætra, 2020c; Smith, 2019), and this is one major obstacle to seeing AI-driven predictive crime fighting a viable path to justice through accountable and inclusive institutions. If we would not care what sort of political systems provided safety and order, however, the construction of AI-based technocracies could arguably be one way to achieve effective institutions and societies (Sætra, 2020c). Doing so would entail radical changes of political structures, and in addition to questions related to whether such changes are viable and desirable, there is also doubt related to whether an AI technocracy would (a) work and (b) not lead to a range of unintended negative effects not related specifically to the efficiency of the political system.

If we turn to the use of AI in general, research has pointed to how AI engenders polarization by how its use is conducive to produce filter bubbles and echo chambers (Sætra, 2019b). In addition to creating dynamics that foster polarization by the way it feeds on unfortunate human psychological mechanisms, it is also instrumental in the creation and dissemination of fake news on social media, etc. (Allcott & Gentzkow, 2017).

Turning to individual notions of justice and inclusive political systems, it is also worth highlighting how AI combined with Big Data enables more effective nudging of individuals (Yeung, 2017). Such nudging can be argued to constitute a form of liberty reducing

Positive Impacts Does AI …	SDG 16	Negative Impacts Does AI …
• Improve access to justice?	+ Micro -	• Allow for more effective government control and manipulation? • Lead to exclusion and discrimination?
• Promote peace and stability in vulnerable areas and groups?	+ Meso -	• Increase polarization and differences between groups?
• Improve to effectiveness of institutions?	+ Macro -	• Reduce transparency and political accountability?
5, 10, 11 11, 17	+ Ripples to - + Ripples from -	17 8, 9

manipulation (Sætra, 2019c), and this realization has made regulators in the European Union proposed the limitation of manipulative use of AI in general and its prohibition in high risk areas, such as education (Europan Commision, 2021). While proponents of nudging have argued that nudging – including AI-based nudging – should only be done for good, and to promote healthy and economically rational choices, etc. (Thaler & Sunstein, 2008), critics have highlighted that it seems far-fetched to believe that those with access to such technologies of manipulation will abstain from using it for other profit-maximizing endeavors which will often harm the individuals targeted (Sætra, 2019c).

While AI has the effects here considered on a national level, it is reasonable to assume that AI-driven polarization will also manifest itself in international relations. The ripple effects of negative AI impacts on SDG 16 will first and foremost challenge and undermine the political action required to reach most of the other SDGs, and goals such as SDG 1, SDG 2, and SDG 17, are particularly vulnerable to these ripple effects.

6

SUSTAINABLE ENVIRONMENTAL DEVELOPMENT

How can computers help save the environment, you might say? The advent of technological change and industrialization is arguably what has led us into the dire straits that we are in, so what sort of techno-optimism is the basis of believing that more technology will help us fix the very same issues? While there is certainly some merit to such misgivings, we will see that artificial intelligence (AI) has some potential to enable the reaching of the environmental goals as well, both directly and indirectly. However, there is also here a flip-side and a danger that AI is used to hinder the reaching of the environmental goals, which are as follows:

- SDG 13 (climate action)
- SDG 14 (life below water)
- SDG 15 (life on land)

SDG 13

Take urgent action to combat climate change and its impacts (United Nations, 2015).

DOI: 10.1201/9781003193180-6

In terms of challenges that threaten life on earth as we know it, few phenomena rival climate change. While the mechanisms behind human-made climate change have been known for a long time, the fact that it is human-made, and that it is a real and pressing issue, has now finally been close to unanimously accepted (IPCC, 2021). The UN's Intergovernmental Panel on Climate Change (IPCC) has delivered numerous reports describing both the science behind climate change, its consequences, and the need for mitigation and adaptation. As stressed by the IPCC, technology plays an important role in adaptation efforts (IPCC, 2014), but it might also play a part in mitigation.

SDG 13 entails efforts to reduce greenhouse gases, mitigate climate change, and also to combat the impacts of climate change. The targets highlight the strengthening of resilience and adaptive capacity, the integration of climate change measures in national policies, strategies, and planning, and the importance of raising awareness and providing good education on the topic. The two targets related to implementation both emphasize the role of the United Nations Framework Convention on Climate Change, the need to mobilize resources from developed countries and other sources to assist developing countries, with a particular focus – once more – on least developed countries and particularly vulnerable groups, mentioning women, youth, and local and marginalized communities. Efforts to reduce emissions are mentioned in the target related to policies, but it is quite clear that SDG 13 strongly favors a focus on *adaptation*.

One way in which AI can help reduce emissions is through its contribution to sustainable infrastructure, industry, and innovation. These indirect effects are potentially significant, but they simultaneously highlight the tension between the various SDGs, as increased industrialization, even if associated with marginally reduced emissions, could conceivably lead to a general increase in emissions. Nevertheless, industrialization and capacity increase in the least well of countries will arguably help increase their capacity to adapt to climate change, and this shows that even within SDG 13 there may be a tension between the desire to radically cut emissions and efforts to adapt to a changing climate.

One key benefit of AI systems is that they excel at optimizing decisions in highly complex environments. Climate policy is arguably one of the most complex policy issues today, and the various direct and indirect effects associated with changes in policy related to infrastructure, mobility, industry, taxes, etc. is arguably too complex for humans to manually figure out, and one prime candidate for seeking the assistance of AI systems. This might entail using AI as decision support while keeping humans in the loop (Sætra, 2022), but it could also entail more drastic measures including considering a limited AI technocracy in which we delegate some decision-making authority to AI systems in order to overcome the limitations of human politicians when it comes to making long-term and politically costly decisions (Sætra, 2020c).

Another potential advantage is the use of AI in the development and deployment of geoengineering. This is a highly controversial approach to the mitigation of and adaptation to climate change based on allowing us to sidestep substantial and radical changes in the sociotechnical system (Samui, 2019), but one that the current trajectory of emissions indicate that we might have to consider more seriously if the efforts to actually combat climate change remain insufficient. Geoengineering is feared for two reasons. First, due to the inevitable unintended effects introduced by meddling with the earth's climate system. Second, because a moral hazard is created when we seriously consider a solution in which we can continue to emit gases way beyond what the carbon sinks can sustainably absorb. The first danger related to unintended effects is one that can be reduced by the use of AI and advanced simulations of the climate system. However, arguing that it could be eliminated would reveal little more than great hubris.

With regard to the negative potential, there is little evidence to suggest that Big Tech and the sort of innovation and economic growth it is built on is particularly green. And while AI can be used to optimize production in terms of reduced emissions or the planning of windmill parks, it can equally well be used to optimize the extraction of oil and gas for maximum profit. These effects are mainly indirect effects related to SDG 8 and SDG 9, but there are also more direct effects related to SDG 13.

Increased attention has recently been devoted to the emissions produced by training natural language models – AI systems – on increasingly large datasets (Brevini, 2020). Such models are integral to the current priorities of the Big Tech companies, and Timnit Gebru, a pioneer in critical AI research, was ousted from Google following co-authorship on an article that highlighted both the questionable useful potential of natural language models, its potential for negative impacts related to, for example, discrimination, and the significant emissions generated by training such models (Bender, Gebru, McMillan-Major, & Shmitchell, 2021). This has led to increased efforts to develop green information technologies (García-Berná et al., 2019), to place data centers in regions with access to renewable energy, to implement best practices related to data center energy efficiency, etc. (EU Technical Expert Group on Sustainable Finance, 2020).

Of some importance is the fact that policymakers tend to view the positive potential of AI and information technology as greater than its negative potential, as indicated by how the new EU taxonomy for sustainable finance does not make reduced emission from data centers a goal, as data-driven solutions for reducing the emissions of greenhouse gases is seen as an important part of reaching the overall goals related to reduced emissions (EU Technical Expert Group on Sustainable Finance, 2020). This points clearly to the need to differentiate between the sustainability of AI in a technical sense and AI used in order to generate or promote sustainable solutions (van Wynsberghe, 2021).

In terms of AI impacts on the macro level, it is necessary to balance any isolated use cases indicating positive AI impacts on climate change mitigation or adoption on the meso or macro level against how AI is tied to Big Tech and efforts to drive conventional economic growth (Brevini, 2020). It seems likely that positive AI impact overall

Positive Impacts Does AI …	SDG 13	Negative Impacts Does AI …
• Provide individuals with means to monitor and reduce their carbon footprint?	+ Micro -	• Introduce moral hazard, by nurturing the idea that technology (such as geoengineering) can fix the problems we face?
• Make adaptation efforts more effective? • Provide companies means to reduce their impacts? • Increase energy effectiveness of data centers, availability of clear energy, etc.?	+ Meso -	• Provide unequal access to adaptation measures? • Allow the advantaged to influence and engineer the climate in ways that benefit them and hurt others?
• Generate new knowledge required to face climate related challenges? • Optimize energy policies and regulation?	+ Macro -	• Produce emissions? • Promote non-democratic politics and open paths toward technocracies?
12, 14, 15 7, 9, 12, 17	+ Ripples to - + Ripples from -	8, 9, 16 8, 9, 16

is premised on a decoupling from this system and the achievement of the goals related to fair and equal access as detailed in SDG 9.

SDG 14

Conserve and sustainably use the oceans, seas and marine resources for sustainable development (United Nations, 2015).

SDG 14 and SDG 15 are both goals for which a number of targets specify actions to be taken by 2020, 2025, and 2030, and some of them are thus partly either achieved or delayed already. Nevertheless, some of the targets are more general, and the overall intentions behind these goals are also of interest on their own seen apart from the specific targets. The 10 targets for SDG 14 specify goals related to the reduction of marine pollution of all kinds, the sustainable management of marine and coastal ecosystems, ocean acidification, over-fishing and unregulated fishing practices, the conservation of 10% of marine and coastal areas, improved regulation and preferential treatment of developing nations and small island developing nations in particular. The means to achieve these goals are to increase scientific knowledge, develop research capacity, and technology transfer. In addition, specific attention is given to giving small-scale artisanal fishers access to marine resources and markets. Finally, international law and regulation of marine resources must be enhanced.

One potential positive application of AI in this context is its use in improved monitoring and surveillance systems for marine and coastal areas and resources, including fish stocks and fishing vessels. Improved insight and control of all marine and coastal activity will enable both nations and the international community to further develop and not least enact stricter and more sustainable policies. Overfishing has led to numerous crises related to diminishing fish stocks, and AI-based monitoring might in theory help prevent the recurrence of, for example, the kind of overfishing that nearly led to the extinction of the North Atlantic cod (Hutchings & Myers, 1994).

Ocean acidification is another topic area, and one potential indirect effect of AI thus comes about through a positive impact on the reduction of greenhouse gas emissions in relation to SDG 13. Ocean acidification is a result of the oceans performing as CO_2 sinks which absorb these gases from the atmosphere, leading to increased acidification and a number of problems for aquatic life, including severe problems for all forms of life dependent on forming various forms of shells. Increased temperatures also lead to coral bleaching, and sea-level rise threatens vast amounts of coastal ecosystems and human settlements (IPCC, 2021).

Reaching SDG 14 depends heavily on the political will of policymakers in both developing and developed nations, and AI in itself will be assumed to have a non-significant impact on the strengthening of such will. The main contribution will be to enable partnerships and treaties based on better monitoring and sanctioning capabilities enabled by AI.

Positive Impacts Does AI ...	SDG 14	Negative Impacts Does AI ...
• Provide individuals with actionable knowledge?	• + Micro -	• Help rogue fishers and others to avoid enforcement?
• Promote the competitiveness of small-scale fishers?	• + Meso -	• Allow groups to circumvent quotas and border controls? • Provide those with resources advantages over those without new technology?
• Improve monitoring and the ability to regulate and enforce regulation?	• + Macro -	• Lead of overuse of resources due to increased effectiveness?
2, 3, 10, 14 9, 13, 17	+ Ripples to - + Ripples from -	10, 17

Furthermore, while AI might be used to monitor fish stocks, for example, this can just as well be used to track and capture fish more effectively by the major players in the fishing industry. It might even help rogue fishers monitor, analyze, and counteract efforts by law enforcement in order to help unlawful fishing and the impoverishment of marine and coastal natural resource stocks.

SDG 15

Protect, restore and promote sustainable use of terrestrial eco-systems, sustainably manage forests, combat desertification, and halt and reverse land degradation and halt biodiversity loss (United Nations, 2015).

While SDG 14 regards coastal and marine ecosystems, SDG 15 encompasses terrestrial and inland water systems as well as all other land-based ecosystems. The targets specify goals related to conser-vation, restoration, and sustainable use of such systems, sustainable use of forest and halting deforestation, combatting desertification, and conserving mountain ecosystem. It also calls for urgent and significant action to preserve natural habitats and stop biodiversity loss, and action to stop poaching and trafficking of vulnerable animals and flora. Furthermore, SDG 15 emphasizes the need for fair and equitable access to the benefits from using genetic resources and the promotion of access to such resources. This is to be achieved by the increased focus on ecosystem and biodiversity values in national and local planning, the mobilization of resources to conserve and sustainably use biodiversity and ecosystems and forest management, and enhancing global support for efforts to combat unlawful poaching and trafficking.

The potential benefits of AI in enabling SDG 15 are once again its potential use in monitoring and generating actionable insight related to the status of ecosystems and biodiversity, and thus improving sustainability through scientific conservationism (Guha, 2012, 2014). Increased information allows for taking appropriate action, for understanding the trajectories we're on, and also for enabling transparency and the possibility for sanctions in treaties and partnerships.

These benefits and non-negligible, but they must also here be seen in conjunction with the opportunity for using the same technologies to extract resources in unsustainable ways, and thus furthering the collapse and degradation of ecosystems and biodiversity. Poachers and companies alike might use satellite imagery and other data in combination with AI systems to exploit natural resources and track and capture wildlife.

As political will and political action are strictly required for achieving the targets for SDG 15, AI impacts are relatively modest, and the main positive impact is provided through improved knowledge and transparency, which can indeed strengthen the political will. Various uses of sensors, databases, and AI systems provide new or deeper knowledge through data on weather, geology, species, satellite imagery, etc., and this data can be used to understand the development of both the health of species, their movement and

Positive Impacts Does AI ...	SDG 15	Negative Impacts Does AI ...
• Allow individuals to engage in efforts to protect and preserve terrestrial ecosystems?	+ Micro -	• Provide new tools for poachers and others seeking to exploit natural resources?
• Promote access to and use of terrestrial ecosystems for the least well-off?	+ Meso -	• Lead to unequitable access to and use of terrestrial ecosystems?
• Improve the foundation of scientific conservationism?	+ Macro -	• Lead to the promotion of geoengineering efforts?
• Provide insight and monitoring capabilities for governments?		• Improve effectiveness of resource extraction and the overuse of resources?
3, 14 9, 17	+ Ripples to - + Ripples from -	10 7, 8, 9, 13

development, and the development of both the biotic and abiotic parts of all ecosystems.

As discussed in relation to SDG 13, AI can also be used to develop and deploy solution which counteracts or replaces whole or parts of natural ecosystems, but efforts akin to geoengineering is not in line with the targets of SDG 15, which calls for preservation and restoration – not alteration or replacement of the natural for the artificial.

7

ASSESSING THE OVERALL IMPACT OF AI

As shown in the three preceding chapters, artificial intelligence (AI) has a wide range of potential positive *and* negative impacts on the various Sustainable Development Goals (SDGs). Leaving it at that is, however, not sufficient, as we must also summarize and try to get to grips with the overall impact of AI. In order to do so I'll return to the main impacts discussed and consider how large of an impact AI can be considered to have on the SDGs. Furthermore, I will consider how likely the purported impacts are to have significant real-life effects. This goes both for the kind of isolated use cases discussed by researchers such as Vinuesa et al. (2020) and for the hypothetical and theoretically based potential impacts discussed throughout this book.

CATEGORIZING THE SDGs BY IMPACTS

As a starting point, it is beneficial to categorize the SDGs by what kind of impact AI has on them in terms of importance and whether the goal "ripples" to other goals. Also, whether the impacts on the goals are mainly direct or indirect. For most goals, there will be both direct and indirect effects, so the following categorization will

DOI: 10.1201/9781003193180-7

Group 1	Top-level goals where AI has high potential impact and significant ripple effects	8, 9
Group 2	Direct effects with ripple effects	3, 4, 11, 16
Group 3	Direct effects without ripple effects	5, 10, 13
Group 4	High impact, but mainly indirect effects	1, 2, 12
Group 5	Minor or no effects	6, 7, 14, 15, 17

necessarily be one of several ways to evaluate the impact of each goal. The categorization below was proposed in Sætra (2021a), and this will serve as the basis for determining which of the goals will receive the most attention in the following analysis of micro-, meso-, and macro-level impacts. The categorization consists of the following five groups of goals:

The top-level goals are SDGs 8 and 9, due to AI system's high impact and direct effects on these goals, in addition to the fact that these goals have major ripple effects on most of the other goals. These goals are considered central for understanding the overall impact of AI on the SDGs, and will thus be particularly emphasized in the following.

Group 2 consists of SDGs 3, 4, 11, and 16, as AI is considered to have a medium impact and a direct effect on these goals, while the goals also have major ripple effects on other goals. As for all the SDGs, AI impact is here both negative and positive, and AI impacts the micro, meso, and macro levels differently, as we will shortly see.

The last group of goals that I consider AI to have significant direct effects on, with medium impact, are SDGs 5, 10, and 13 in group 3. For these goals, the ripple effects of AI impact will most likely not lead to significant ripple effects on other goals, and they are thus considered to be marginally less central in this context than the goals in groups 1 and 2.

Groups 4 and 5 consist of the rest of the SDGs, and these goals will mainly be relevant because of the ripple effects of AI impact from the other SDGs. The goals in group 4, for which I consider the indirect AI impact to be high, are SDGs 1, 2, and 12. The remaining goals, SDGs 6, 7, 14, 15, and 17, are arguably only marginally impacted by AI, and they will thus not receive much attention in the following discussion.

AI IMPACT ON THE MICRO, MESO, AND MACRO LEVELS

The preceding chapters contain the discussions of each SDG, and the question of how AI impacts the SDGs overall, and particularly how impacts can be understood by distinguishing between micro-, meso-, and macro-level effects, must now be answered. The problem with previous accounts of AI impacts on the SDGs, for example, Vinuesa et al. (2020), is that they are often highly quantitative and empirical in nature. Furthermore, as much of the research done thus far is published in article format, the required space to really explore the intricacies of the SDGs and their interdependencies have not been available. Even a book such as this is arguably far too short to do justice to the complexities of both AI and the SDGs, but it nevertheless provides valuable opportunities to do more than what can be done in far fewer pages.

In addition to the lack of space, too little attention has previously been paid to impacts that are not easily quantifiable and those that have not been empirically demonstrated. While numbers and demonstrable impacts are indeed important, the main contribution of this book is to add qualitative insight and considerations of theoretically deduced potential long-term and indirect effects of AI. While, for example, the impact of AI-driven inequality on individuals may be difficult to demonstrate empirically, such impacts can be theoretically deduced from an analysis of other phenomena. While such impacts are uncertain, and the precise degree of impact will be unknown, it must be remembered that the same caveats must be carried into any analysis in which proofs-of-concept and demonstrations of AI potential in small-scale or even experimental settings. Vinuesa et al. (2020), for example, acknowledge that much of the "evidence" they use to present AI as an enabler of the SDGs is based on experimental closed systems. The real world, however, is anything but a closed system (Bhaskar, 2013; Davidsen, 2010), and humility with regards to the precision and validity of any measurement of impact, and particularly the generalization from closed systems to open systems, is strictly necessary for any serious analysis of AI impacts on the SDGs. By broadening the arsenal of permissible evidence to also include theoretical considerations regarding the sociotechnical system, for example, this allows me to explore the linkage between the various SDGs and technology's role in the economic, social, and political systems (Barley, 2020).

Another requirement for a useful analysis of AI impacts is a willingness to examine the *degree* of impact AI has on each SDG and/or target. Some have simply treated impact as positive, non-existent, or negative. This, however, leads to a situation in which a potential minuscule positive impact seemingly nullifies or balances out a *significant* negative contribution, as they are counted equally – one positive and one negative effect. As seen above, I have rated impact by degree, and will disregard any impacts deemed insignificant in order to focus attention on what is most likely the most significant impacts of AI.

Finally, a major pitfall for those who require evidence and quantification for any impact to be counted is blindness to how AI is a double-edged sword, as shown throughout the preceding chapters. When someone proves that AI can be used to track and analyze the movement of fish stocks, for example, and argue that this is a proof that AI can be used to save and sustainably manage coastal and marine resources, any diligent researcher must then point out that the demonstrated capability of this AI system can, for example, also be used to exploit the same resources unsustainably. A foundational choice in this book is to never assume that any developer, owner, or deployer of AI systems have strictly good intentions, as these systems can be used in theory by any actors, for any purpose. At least until something changes drastically in the landscape of AI development. One example of research that acknowledges the dual nature of AI is reported in Truby (2020), who demonstrates that while AI can be used for detecting and combatting money laundering, it can just as easily be used to make money laundering more effective and to avoid anti-money laundering efforts. One benefit of acknowledging the multi-purpose nature of AI is that much of the evidence in existence really serves as proof of what they explicitly state – some positive proofs can be used as proof of negative potential, and vice versa.

With these preliminaries out of the way, it is time to explore the main impacts on each of the three levels.

MICRO-LEVEL AI IMPACTS

The micro level is mainly considered to be related to the effects on individuals and small groups. Distributional effects and relative impact of AI – the kind of impact that affects the differences between groups and individuals – will mainly be considered as part of the meso and macro levels. However, one micro-level impact which cannot be distinguished from distributional aspects is the impact AI has on relative poverty and SDG 1. One might argue that only absolute poverty determines a person's abilities to get a hold of food and other relevant resources, but the SDGs are based on the notion that relative differences matter as well. Furthermore, while absolute poverty is clearly relevant for the micro level, relative poverty can also deprive people of the chance to succeed in life, as other people's relative advantage will be of importance in a wide range of settings. While I stated in Chapter 4 that AI-driven economic growth might be argued to reduced absolute poverty, I have simultaneously argued that the kind of growth we have seen associated with AI thus far is susceptible to increase relative poverty. These effects are the indirect effects of AI stemming from SDG 8, and how we evaluate the overall impact on SDG 1 (no poverty) will thus depend on how we weigh absolute vs. relative poverty. The other goals in group 4 – SDG 2 (zero hunger) and SDG 12 (responsible consumption and production) – are also placed in this group because of their indirect effects on other goals. Economic growth and any decrease in absolute poverty which is not simultaneously accompanied by higher prices or increased difficulties of getting access to food, is one area where AI can have a high positive impact on the micro level, as fewer individuals will be exposed to hunger in such a setting. This will simultaneously have positive indirect effects on SDG 3 (good health).

Responsible consumption and production are areas where the micro-level effects related to increased monitoring and analysis-capabilities leading to increased awareness and control are direct. Meanwhile, the meso- and macro-level effects will mainly be indirect effects from SDG 9 (innovation and industry) and partly the ripple effects of the micro-level impact. Using AI to increase awareness is considered to have a positive effect on SDG 12, but the indirect effects on SDG 8 and SDG 9 could work in opposite directions, as economic growth might drive consumption in general, while innovation could make such consumption less unsustainable. The same considerations go for AI impacts related to increased awareness of a person's carbon footprint, in relation to SDG 13 (climate action). The effects of individual choices are clearly not insignificant, but the number of individuals who would have to drastically change their behavior exceeds what can be expected to follow from increased awareness promoted by AI. In order to reach the goals related to SDG 13, then, changes on the meso and macro levels are required. Furthermore, as discussed in the previous chapter, AI might also drive consumption and thus lead to increased carbon footprints for individuals in contexts where AI-infused products lead to increased needs for updates and shorter product life cycles.

SDG 8 will also have micro-level effects, and while the targets related to economic growth will mainly be relevant for the meso and macro levels, issues related to the decency of work clearly impact the micro-level. These effects will be both positive and negative, as AI can be used to improve safety and the mental and physical toll of work for many, but it can also lead to automation which reduces opportunities for decent work. When coupled with employee surveillance it can also be used to make working conditions less decent as liberty is threatened when employees are increasingly able to both control and manipulate their employees (Manokha, 2020; Sætra, 2021b). This also relates to the micro-level effects relevant to SDG

5 and 10 in group 3, which focus on gender equality and reduced inequalities in general. While AI systems, either related to employment, hiring, etc., or other domains such as the ability to get a loan, get out on bail, etc., will for some individuals potentially improve their chances of what they label good outcomes, it has also been thoroughly documented that such AI systems are susceptible to bias and discriminatory outcomes. Such instances of discrimination constitute micro-level impacts relevant for a wide range of SDGs, but particularly SDG 5 and SDG 10. However, SDG 16, which relates to access to justice and safety is also clearly important for any discussion of micro-level impact, and the use of AI-based policing and processes of the justice system might improve the situation for some, these systems are also susceptible to the just discussed bias and discriminatory outcomes. The overall balance of these impacts is up for debate, however, and if efforts to combat bias in AI systems succeed, the overall impact on the micro level might be positive, as human-based decision-making is replaced or corrected by less biased AI systems.

The use of AI in an educational context shows a positive potential related to SDG 4, but also partly to the context of work and SDG 8. While remote access to quality education is not dependent on AI, the use of AI might provide higher quality remote education through the personalization it allows for (Sætra, 2021d). As the benefits of access to such learning systems are particularly valuable to those living in places where school infrastructure and access to good teachers are restricted, these effects seem particularly relevant for enabling SDG 4. While positive, it must also be noted that the use of AI in education involves using AI in a context where children and young people are exposed to it, and particular care must thus be exerted in such high-risk applications (European Commision, 2021).

Finally, the use of AI in the context of smart cities will provide the individuals in such cities with access to infrastructure innovations that might ease their lives and improve the services they use, in addition to making cities safer, and more navigable. This is all achieved through the combination of the collection of Big Data and AI-based analysis, and as such, these benefits are also associated with potential negative impacts related to increased surveillance and the potential bias inherent in such AI systems.

These are the micro-level impacts I consider to be most significant, but there will clearly also be other impacts that could arguably be included here. This analysis must thus be considered a starting point for those wanting to evaluate the micro-level impacts of any particular AI system or application.

MESO-LEVEL AI IMPACTS

Moving from individuals and small groups, the meso level entails considerations regarding larger organizations and groups, including the relationships between such groups (Jonsson, 2016). As this book focuses on the SDGs, a global scope is required, and this entails that the national level, which will often be considered the macro level, will here be considered part of the meso level, as the differences and relationships between countries occur at an intermediate level with regards to the global political level.

SDG 8 and SDG 9 are the top-level goals, and AI has important meso-level impacts related to these goals. As discussed at some length, the nature of the economic growth engendered by – or associated with – AI is instrumental for determining the relative strength, competitiveness, and opportunities of groups. My position has been that AI thus far has not been conducive to disproportionately favoring the least well off in terms of developing and least developed countries. On the contrary, AI based on data and proprietary solutions are susceptible to exacerbate differences between groups and nations. As such, the meso-level effects related to SDG 8 are at least partly negative. Furthermore, these negative effects ripple to just about all the other SDGs, as fundamental premises for the SDGs are reduced inequalities and a particular focus on developing and least developed countries. As previously discussed, differences between classes are now perhaps even more important than differences between nations, but inequalities in the age of Big Tech have grown in both regards.

While class and nations are very large groups, AI also impacts groups on lower levels, and in relation to SDG 8, it is particularly important to examine the impacts on the power distribution between employees and employers. While employers might use AI-based systems to improve their work situations, and potentially to resist potential attempts to breach workplace regulation etc., I argue that increased access to data and increased use of AI-based systems disproportionately benefit employers. This is because employers both increase their means of surveillance and control, and the use of AI for automation also entails shifts in bargaining power in favor of those who can implement, or threaten to implement, solutions that automate work previously performed by humans.

The impacts on SDG 9 resemble SDG 8 in how any progress related to innovation, infrastructure, and industry all lead to shifts in the distribution of power and capabilities between groups and nations. Unlike SDG 8, however, there is a broader scope for arguing that the innovations related to foundational science, more effective infrastructure solutions, or more effective management of existing infrastructure have the potential for significantly improving the situation for those most in need of it. For this to occur, however, the required political will must be fostered, and decisions to share technology and facilitate the spread of innovation and help build infrastructure based on AI must be taken and followed through by developed countries. While AI creates the conditions for this to happen, the actual impact depends on both this potential *and* what is done with it. Without substantial efforts to spread and disseminate benefits related to SDG 9, AI might lead to a situation in which innovation and infrastructure development disproportionally benefit those with the resources to develop and use such systems. Making such a situation even worse is the fact that infrastructure also encompasses the information technology required to develop and use AI-based solutions effectively. With regard to the industry part of SDG 9, there are distributional considerations similar to those relevant for SDG 8 in play, and in order to AI have positive meso-level effects it must lead to inclusive and sustainable industry and this relates once again to the power relations between employer and employees and also to issues related to automation.

As the preceding considerations demonstrate, the reason I call SDG 8 and SDG 9 top-level goals is because these will have major ripple effects on all the other SDGs. We have seen that all of the goals consist of targets that relate to the distribution of benefits not only between developed and developing countries, but also between people in general (SDG 10) and between the genders more specifically (SDG 5).

With regard to SDG 16 and SDG 17, AI can potentially enable a shift in the relationship between, and relative capabilities and power of, the government and private-sector corporations, and this is potentially of great importance. This relates particularly to how access to data and the means of surveillance and intelligence through Big Data and AI has shifted and enabled private-sector actors to become major – if not the major – actors capable of large-scale surveillance and the use of the information gathered through surveillance (Sætra, 2019a). AI-enabled policing and government intelligence gathering are increasingly dependent on private companies for data and access to the best solutions, and this leads to a situation in which government loses relative power. Furthermore, as the government is not in full control of the technologies used, they might also be unable to effectively transfer technology to developing nations, unless this means that developing countries are to be given access to the solutions of private companies from developed countries. This will, however, not be in line with the SDG targets which call for local development and capacity-building.

A further issue related to SDG 16 (politics and institutions) is how private companies have gained relative power over political processes. Facebook and Google, for example, use AI to curate and distribute news and ads to a majority of voters in modern societies, and much attention has been paid to how they and other companies thus gain massive political power without the regulation associated with traditional media. In addition to this, social media and the internet enables other threats to political institutions and political processes, as the government is increasingly unable to control and monitor how both domestic and foreign actors use technology to influence voters and political processes. AI is part of this threat as, for example, automated "bots" are designed to pose as regular citizens in order to spread disinformation or eschew public opinion, and also in the creation and dissemination of both fake news and deep fakes.

The key questions related to how AI indirectly enable or prevent inequality and the role of the least well off are covered in the tables associated with each SDG in the preceding chapters. As with the micro-level goals, any comprehensive analysis of a particular AI system or application will allow for deducing more specific questions, considerations, and evaluations of meso-level impacts related to the specific topic evaluated. The considerations in this chapter are mainly intended to form the basis of such analyses.

MACRO-LEVEL AI IMPACTS

The macro-level impacts entail the broader and long-term impacts related to the global economic and political systems, and I'll focus in particular on how these changes – which are necessarily hypothetical and unsure – relate to the need for political action in order to ensure that AI's overall impact is to enable the reaching of the SDGs. This also means that SDGs 16 and 17, which relate most specifically to politics and partnerships, are considered key for understanding the impacts of AI, promoting the beneficial impacts, and mitigating the undesirable ones.

The environmental dimension of sustainability has received little attention in the discussion of micro-level and meso-level impacts, as the impacts on SDGs 13, 14, and 15 are mainly related to macro-level impacts on economic or political activity. Economic growth based on traditional models of extracting natural resources can be linked to the use of AI for more effective extraction and unsustainable use of these resources. As should be clear to all by now, traditional and existing regulations have not been able to sufficiently restrict the unsustainable use of natural resources and the emission of climate gases, and as long as this is not remedied, economic actors will continue to have incentives to use AI to gain short-term profits which inhibit the reaching of all the environmental goals. One potential counterweight to this is the micro-level effects related to increased awareness and potential grass-roots mobilization against actors inhibiting the environmental goals. Any AI contribution on the micro-level will change the incentives for economic actors somewhat, but it seems unlikely that the impact of AI itself on this area will cause sufficient shifts in public opinion to the inhibition of the environmental goals where regulations allow for unsustainable activity for short-term profit. We thus require political action as well, and partnerships, which I return to below in the discussion of SDG 16 and SDG 17.

The key to understanding the overall impact of AI is to consider how AI impacts the trajectory of economic growth and innovation, and how political activity and human activity, in general, is likely to change this trajectory.

A recurring topic throughout the book is that AI has thus far been associated with economic growth, but not with inclusive and sustainable economic growth. As long as AI disproportionately favors those with the required infrastructure, and by this I here include computing infrastructure and the data required for most current data-driven AI solutions, it will have negative macro-level impacts on SDG 8 and SDG 9 directly, and on all of the others indirectly. This can, however, change if political action is taken to strengthen efforts by developing countries to transfer technology to and support developing and least developed countries. However, this cannot be based on exporting ready-made solutions alone, or simply granting access to proprietary systems owned or controlled by developed countries. In the context of the SDGs, proper transfer and support entail making technology accessible but also aiding in the development of the infrastructure required to make use of the technology in question (SDG 9).

One long-term impact of the use of AI is the increasing digitalization and datafication of all aspects of economic activity and society in general. Any impacts of AI – both positive and negative – will be positively associated with this development, meaning that the positive impact will become more significant, and also that the negative impacts will become more severe. This means that any development toward increased digitalization, and not just smart cities, but smart nations, and a smart world, will have to be accompanied with increased efforts to mitigate the negative potential of AI. This can occur through activity related to SDG 9. The democratization of AI and the infrastructure used to develop and apply AI-based solutions can both not only help reduce bias and negative effects related to disproportionate representation and limited geographical and social participation in development, but also help to reduce the inequality generated when the use of AI is restricted to those already well off.

As discussed in relation to the meso level, the shift in power between the public and the private sectors – in favor of the latter – could potentially threaten SDG 16 and our ability to build effective, accountable, and inclusive institutions at all levels. This relates particularly to the capabilities of government to secure the rule of law (target 16.3), as we might find ourselves in a situation in which the private sector contributes to a decrease in violence and improve law enforcement as detailed in several targets, while simultaneously decreasing transparency and accountability as the government is marginalized.

SDG 17 relates to partnerships, and all areas of interest under this target – finance, technology, capacity-building, trade, and systemic issues – will be influenced by the developments related to economic growth and the increasing power of large corporations. Partnerships both for financing, harmonization of national laws and regulation, and transfer of technology are essential for reaching all of the SDGs. However, AI is at best a relatively insignificant enabler of such partnerships through its use in enabling transparency and monitoring of agreements, and at worst a major obstacle to such partnerships.

One particularly troubling development currently debated is the question of whether AI is the subject matter of a new "cold war". Some argue that it is, as nations and corporations struggle for preeminence in the data-based and AI-driven world of tomorrow

(Zhang et al., 2021), while others do their best to alleviate such worries (Bryson & Malikova, 2021). Regardless of whether the US and China, for example, are in a conflict related to the relative power of their major technology companies, the more impact AI has, both in general and related to the SDGs, the more likely it will be that nations and economic actors will struggle for relative advantage. Private actors see great market power and monetary rewards in leading data-driven AI, but governments are also increasingly aware of the power they get, or give up, if others are given the opportunity to gather data on their citizens and exert AI-based influence in their territories.

Another potential source of conflict of AI pre-eminence is the potential military use of AI. Campaigns against "killer robots" abound, but far less spectacular use of AI in existing technology, airplanes, missile guidance systems, etc. is already in place and ensures that AI leadership is and will remain important. As such, AI will play a key role in any consideration of the development of the economic and political systems. While AI has a limited direct positive effect on SDG 17, it is a potential source of great conflict. Partnerships and regulation that promote either restriction of data-gathering or the use of AI-based data-driven solutions, or instead creates new solutions in which both AI systems and data is openly accessible to all, might change this rather ominous evaluation, and should thus be a key focus area in future research and regulatory work.

THE LIMITS OF THE SDG FRAMEWORK

After considering the impacts of AI on the SDGs, it only remains to remind the reader that an evaluation based on these goals is inextricably linked to the strengths and limitations of the SDG framework. The strengths have been shown by how they enforce a broad consideration of economic, social, and environmental issues, and also how they emphasize and necessitate consideration of sociotechnical systems and how technology will have a wide range of diverse effects on different levels.

However, there are also things that might be of great importance that are not covered by the SDGs, and any complete analysis of AI impact in general – not AI impact on the SDGs – will have to be based on other frameworks as well. First of all, the SDG is based on the premise that economic growth is desirable and good, but this in itself is the subject matter of intense debate, particularly between proponents of economic growth and those emphasizing the need for drastic and immediate action to mitigate the degradation of the climate and life on land and below water.

In addition to a fundamental faith in growth, the SDGs are also based on a foundational techno-optimism, as most of the SDGs discuss how technology can be used to reach the various goals. However, as shown throughout this book, technology will also often be the cause of challenges to sustainability, and some will even argue that technological development is the main cause of the environmental challenges we face today. The SDGs are thus in a certain sense based on a shallow form of environmentalism (Næss, 1989), as they focus more on mitigating and tweaking the main consequences of human activity, rather than changing the very economic and political systems arguably giving rise to these consequences. In the vocabulary of Arne Næss (1989), a *deeper* approach would entail a readiness to evaluate the very foundations of human societies in order to allow for the possibility that radical and foundational changes are what is required, and not technological ad hoc fixes that are mainly directed at the symptoms of the current ordering of human activity.

In addition, the SDGs entail a very limited focus on individual-level effects related to individual rights and, for example, liberty. While distributional considerations and discrimination are heavily emphasized, other effects of AI on individuals require an additional framework. The use of facial recognition and surveillance might, for example, have negative effects on all, regardless of who or where they are (Sætra, 2021b), but the SDGs require us to link any negative impact from this technology to injustice and discrimination or oppression of particular groups. Other moral and legal theories might thus be of use when considering overall AI impact, and the

Universal Declaration of Human Rights constitutes one such frame-work. It might also be noted that the SDGs are based on human rights, so drawing on these rights is also clearly in alignment with the overall intentions of the SDGs. Issues related to a loss of privacy, loss of autonomy, manipulation, etc., can more easily be understood through an individual rights-based approach, and will thus serve as an important supplement to the SDGs.

8

CONCLUSION

I'm sure a lot of people expected a tutorial on how artificial intelligence (AI) will save us all when they picked up a book titled *AI for the Sustainable Development Goals*. If you were one of them, I hope you were not too disappointed when you found out that this book is at least as much about how AI threatens the reaching of the Sustainable Development Goals (SDGs) as it has been about how it enables us to reach them. There are several reasons for my choice of focus, and I'll briefly reiterate them here.

First, it is only too easy to gather a number of success stories and argue that AI has the potential to enable the reaching of many of the SDGs. Both easy, and true, but not the whole story. AI does indeed have much positive potential, but it is also associated with a significant amount of hype and mystery. There is consequently a real possibility that such sunshine stories about how AI will solve all our problems will lead the non-technical general public to lose sight of the real scope of the challenges we face. Because, as I have argued, some of the positive potential of AI is real, but quite minor. Simultaneously, and more concerning, is the significant negative potential also associated with AI. I hope I have managed to convince you that AI has both positive and negative potential, and that the future impact of AI depends on the political and individual choices we as consumers, developers, bureaucrats, and voters make when we build, regulate, and use AI systems.

DOI: 10.1201/9781003193180-8

Second, if we focus exclusively on the demonstrated positive potential of AI, we miss the chance of preempting the potential negative impacts of AI. This can be done through raising general awareness, political action, or industry self-regulation. It is also worthwhile to point out that AI might in fact be used to counteract "its own" negative impacts once we become aware of them. Even those who disagree with me when it comes to the negative potential of AI have little to lose from supporting a development trajectory in which the precautionary principle is used to make sure that AI systems are built to prevent, detect, and counteract potential negative SDG-related impacts.

The SDGs are intended to *transform our world* (United Nations, 2015) – for the better, and in a sustainable manner. While it is useful to examine how AI can contribute to the reaching of the SDGs, this book has also clearly demonstrated the potential for using the SDGs to evaluate the social, environmental, and economic consequences of AI. This makes the SDGs a useful complement to the traditional frameworks often used in AI ethics, as they explicitly and without compromise drive home the message that sustainable development is not just about isolated use cases. It is about how our technologies and social institutions either help reduce or exacerbate the differences between individuals, groups, and nations. I have shown that AI can be used to both improve and worsen the situation and that all aspects of AI – the infrastructure it is built on, who develops it, who owns it, who has access to it, who uses it, and what it is used for – must be understood and addressed in order to ensure that we get AI for the SDGs.

REFERENCES

Allcott, H., & Gentzkow, M. (2017). Social media and fake news in the 2016 election. *Journal of Economic Perspectives*, 31(2), 211–236.

Anderson, E. (2017). *Private Government: How Employers Rule Our Lives (and Why We Don't Talk About It)*. Princeton: Princeton University Press.

Appel, M., Marker, C., & Gnambs, T. (2020). Are social media ruining our lives? A review of meta-analytic evidence. *Review of General Psychology*, 24(1), 60–74.

Barley, S. R. (2020). *Work and Technological Change*. Oxford, USA: Oxford University Press.

Bender, E. M., Gebru, T., McMillan-Major, A., & Shmitchell, S. (2021). On the dangers of stochastic parrots: Can language models be too big. *Proceedings of FAccT*. doi:10.1145/3442188.3445922.

Bhaskar, R. (2013). General introduction. In M. Archer, A. Collier, T. Lawson, & A. Norrie (Eds.), *Critical Realism: Essential Readings*. London: Routledge.

Bishop, C. M. (2006). *Pattern Recognition and Machine Learning*. New York: Springer.

Bregman, R. (2017). *Utopia for Realists: And How We Can Get There*. London: Bloomsbury Publishing.

Brevini, B. (2020). Black boxes, not green: Mythologizing artificial intelligence and omitting the environment. *Big Data & Society*, 7(2). doi:10.1177/2053951720935141.

Brundtland, G. H., Khalid, M., Agnelli, S., Al-Athel, S., & Chidzero, B. (1987). Our common future. New York, 8.

Bryson, J. J., & Malikova, H. (2021). Is there an AI cold war? *Global Perspectives*, 2(1), 24803.

Buolamwini, J., & Gebru, T. (2018). *Gender shades: Intersectional accuracy disparities in commercial gender classification*. Paper presented at the Conference on fairness, accountability and transparency.

Chancel, L. (2019). Ten facts about inequality in advanced economies. *WID.World Working Paper* (2019/15).

Chui, M., Harryson, M., Manyika, J., Roberts, R., Chung, R., van Heteren, A., & Nel, P. (2018). Notes from the AI frontier: Applying AI for social good. *McKinsey Global Institute*.

Coalition for Critical Technology. (2020). Abolish the #TechToPrisonPipeline. Retrieved from https://medium.com/@CoalitionForCriticalTechnology/abolish-the-techtoprisonpipeline-9b5b14366b16

Coeckelbergh, M. (2020). *AI Ethics*. Cambridge, MA: MIT Press.

Culpepper, P. D., & Thelen, K. (2020). Are we all Amazon primed? Consumers and the politics of platform power. *Comparative Political Studies*, 53(2), 288–318. doi:10.1177/0010414019852687.

D'Alfonso, S., Santesteban-Echarri, O., Rice, S., Wadley, G., Lederman, R., Miles, C., …, Alvarez-Jimenez, M. (2017). Artificial intelligence-assisted online social therapy for youth mental health. *Frontiers in Psychology*, 8, 796.

Danaher, J. (2019). *Automation and Utopia: Human Flourishing in a World without Work*. Cambridge, MA: Harvard University Press.

Davidsen, B.-I. (2010). Towards a critical realist-inspired economic methodology. *Journal of Philosophical Economics*, 3(2), 74–96.

de Sousa, W. G., de Melo, E. R. P., Bermejo, P. H. D. S., Farias, R. A. S., & Gomes, A. O. (2019). How and where is artificial intelligence in the public sector going? A literature review and research agenda. *Government Information Quarterly*, 36(4), 101392. doi:10.1016/j.giq.2019.07.004.

Di Vaio, A., Palladino, R., Hassan, R., & Escobar, O. (2020). Artificial intelligence and business models in the sustainable development goals perspective: A systematic literature review. *Journal of Business Research*, 121, 283–314. doi:10.1016/j.jbusres.2020.08.019.

Dignum, V. (2019). *Responsible Artificial Intelligence: How to Develop and Use AI in a Responsible Way*. Cham: Springer.

Engström, E., & Strimling, P. (2020). Deep learning diffusion by infusion into preexisting technologies–Implications for users and society at large. *Technology in Society*, 63, 101396.

EU Technical expert group on sustainable finance. (2020). *Technical annex to the TEG final report on the EU taxonomy*. Retrieved from https://ec.europa.eu/info/sites/default/files/business_economy_euro/banking_and_finance/documents/200309-sustainable-finance-teg-final-report-taxonomy-annexes_en.pdf

Europan Commision. (2021). Europe fit for the Digital Age: Commission proposes new rules and actions for excellence and trust in Artificial Intelligence [Press release]. Retrieved from https://ec.europa.eu/commission/presscorner/detail/en/IP_21_1682.

Floridi, L., Cowls, J., Beltrametti, M., Chatila, R., Chazerand, P., Dignum, V., ... Rossi, F. (2018). AI4People—an ethical framework for a good AI society: Opportunities, risks, principles, and recommendations. *Minds and Machines*, 28(4), 689–707. doi: 10.1007/s11023-018-9482-5.

Foer, F. (2017). *World Without Mind*. New York: Random House.

Gabriel, I., & Gauri, V. (2019). Towards a new global narrative for the sustainable development goals. In J. Walker, A. Pekmezovic, & G. Walker (Eds.), *Sustainable Development Goals: Harnessing Business to Achieve the SDGs through Finance, Technology, and Law Reform*. West Sussex: John Wiley & Sons Ltd.

García-Berná, J. A., Fernández-Alemán, J. L., Carrillo de Gea, J. M., Nicolás, J., Moros, B., Toval, A., ... Calero, C. (2019). Green IT and sustainable technology development: Bibliometric overview. *Sustainable Development*, 27(4), 613–636.

Gillespie, T. (2010). The politics of 'platforms'. *New Media & Society*, 12(3), 347–364. doi:10.1177/1461444809342738.

Guha, R. (2012). Environmental justice. In D. Schmidtz (Ed.), *Environmental Ethics: What Really Matters, What Really Works*. New York: Oxford University Press.

Guha, R. (2014). *Environmentalism: A Global History*. UK: Penguin.

Heaven, D. (2019). Two minds are better than one. *New Scientist*, 243(3244), 38–41.

Herrman, J. (2019, November 13th). We're Stuck With the Tech Giants. But They're Stuck With Each Other. *New York Times Magazine*. Retrieved from https://www.nytimes.com/interactive/2019/11/13/magazine/internet-platform.html.

Huang, J., Pray, C., & Rozelle, S. (2002). Enhancing the crops to feed the poor. *Nature*, 418(6898), 678–684.

Hutchings, J. A., & Myers, R. A. (1994). What can be learned from the collapse of a renewable resource? Atlantic cod, Gadus morhua, of Newfoundland and Labrador. *Canadian Journal of Fisheries and Aquatic Sciences*, 51(9), 2126–2146.

International Telecommunication Union. (2020). *United 4 Smart Sustainable Cities.* Retrieved from https://www.itu.int/en/ITU-T/ssc/united/Pages/default.aspx.

IPCC. (2014). Summary for policymakers. In *Climate Change 2014: Impacts, Adaption, and Vulnerability* (Vol. AR5). Cambridge: Cambridge University Press.

IPCC. (2021). *Climate Change 2021: The Physical Science Basis. Contribution of Working Group I to the Sixth Assessment Report of the Intergovernmental Panel on Climate Change.* Retrieved from https://www.ipcc.ch/report/ar6/wg1/

Jonsson, I. (2016). *The Political Economy of Innovation and Entrepreneurship: From Theories to Practice.* London: Routledge.

Khakurel, J., Penzenstadler, B., Porras, J., Knutas, A., & Zhang, W. (2018). The rise of artificial intelligence under the lens of sustainability. *Technologies*, 6(4), 100. doi:10.3390/technologies6040100.

Koestler, A. (1967). *The Ghost in the Machine.* London: Pan Books Ltd.

Laney, D. (2001). 3D data management: Controlling data volume, velocity and variety. *META Group Research Note*, 6(70), 1.

Latouche, S. (2009). *Farewell to Growth.* Cambridge: Polity.

Le Blanc, D. (2015). Towards integration at last? The sustainable development goals as a network of targets. *Sustainable Development*, 23(3), 176–187.

Lupton, D. (2016). *The Quantified Self.* Hoboken, NJ: John Wiley & Sons.

Lupton, D. (2019). *Data Selves: More-than-Human Perspectives.* Hoboken, NJ: John Wiley & Sons.

Manokha, I. (2020). The implications of digital employee monitoring and people analytics for power relations in the workplace. *Surveillance & Society*, 18(4), 540–554. doi:10.24908/ss.v18i4.13776.

Marcus, G., & Davis, E. (2019). *Rebooting AI: Building Artificial Intelligence We Can Trust.* New York: Pantheon.

Mills, S. (2020). # DeleteFacebook: From popular protest to a new model of platform capitalism? *New Political Economy.* doi:10.1080/13563467.2020.1858777.

Müller, V. C. (2020). Ethics of Artificial Intelligence and Robotics. In E. N. Zalta (Ed.), *Stanford Encyclopedia of Philosophy* (Summer 2020 Edition). Retrieved from https://plato.stanford.edu/entries/ethics-ai/

Müller, V. C. (Ed.) (2016). *Risks of Artificial Intelligence*. Boca Raton, FL: CRC Press.

Næss, A. (1989). *Ecology, Community and Lifestyle: Outline of an Ecosophy*. Cambridge: Cambridge University Press.

Nerini, F. F., Sovacool, B., Hughes, N., Cozzi, L., Cosgrave, E., Howells, M., … Milligan, B. (2019). Connecting climate action with other Sustainable Development Goals. *Nature Sustainability*, 2(8), 674–680.

Nilsson, M., Griggs, D., & Visbeck, M. (2016). Policy: Map the interactions between Sustainable Development Goals. *Nature*, 534(7607), 320–322.

Noble, S. U. (2018). *Algorithms of Oppression: How Search Engines Reinforce Racism*. New York: New York University Press.

Nwana, H. S. (1990). Intelligent tutoring systems: an overview. *Artificial Intelligence Review*, 4(4), 251–277.

Parker, K., Salas, M., & Nwosu, V. C. (2010). High fructose corn syrup: production, uses and public health concerns. *Biotechnology and Molecular Biology Reviews*, 5(5), 71–78.

Pekmezovic, A. (2019). The UN and goal setting: From the MDGs to the SDGs. In J. Walker, A. Pekmezovic, & G. Walker (Eds.), *Sustainable Development Goals: Harnessing Business to Achieve the SDGs through Finance, Technology, and Law Reform*. West Sussex: John Wiley & Sons Ltd.

Pelto, P. J. (1987). *The Snowmobile Revolution: Technology and Social Change in the Arctic*. Long Grove, IL: Waveland Press Inc.

Petit, N. (2020). *Big Tech and the Digital Economy: The Moligopoly Scenario*. Oxford: Oxford University Press.

Piketty, T. (2014). *Capital in the Twenty-First Century* (A. Goldhammer, Trans.). Cambridge: The Belknap Press of Harvard University Press.

Pistono, F. (2012). *Robots Will Steal Your Job, But that's Ok: How to Survive the Economic Collapse and Be Happy*. Federico Pistono.

Raney, T. (2006). Economic impact of transgenic crops in developing countries. *Current Opinion in Biotechnology*, 17(2), 174–178.

Ritchie, H., Roser, M., Mispy, J., & Ortiz-Ospina, E. (2021). Measuring progress towards the Sustainable Development Goals. Retrieved from SDG-Tracker. org.

Russell, S., & Norvig, P. (2014). *Artificial Intelligence: A Modern Approach* (Third ed.). Essex: Pearson.

Sachs, J. D. (2012). From millennium development goals to sustainable development goals. *The Lancet, 379*(9832), 2206–2211. doi:10.1016/S0140-6736(12)60685-0.

Sætra, H. S. (2018). Science as a vocation in the era of big data: The philosophy of science behind big data and humanity's continued part in science. *Integrative Psychological and Behavioral Science, 52*(4), 508–522.

Sætra, H. S. (2019a). Freedom under the gaze of Big Brother: Preparing the grounds for a liberal defence of privacy in the era of Big Data. *Technology in Society, 58*, 101160.

Sætra, H. S. (2019b). The tyranny of perceived opinion: Freedom and information in the era of big data. *Technology in Society, 59*, 101155. doi:10.1016/j.techsoc.2019.101155.

Sætra, H. S. (2019c). When nudge comes to shove: Liberty and nudging in the era of big data. *Technology in Society, 59*, 101130. doi:10.1016/j.techsoc.2019.04.006.

Sætra, H. S. (2020a). First, they came for the old and demented. *Human Arenas*, 1–19. doi:10.1007/s42087-020-00125-7.

Sætra, H. S. (2020b). Privacy as an aggregate public good. *Technology in Society, 63*, 101422. doi:10.1016/j.techsoc.2020.101422.

Sætra, H. S. (2020c). A shallow defence of a technocracy of artificial intelligence: Examining the political harms of algorithmic governance in the domain of government. *Technology in Society, 62*, 101283.

Sætra, H. S. (2021a). AI in context and the sustainable development goals: Factoring in the unsustainability of the sociotechnical system. *Sustainability, 13*(4). doi:10.3390/su13041738.

Sætra, H. S. (2021b). *Big Data's Threat to Liberty*. Cambridge, MA: Academic Press.

Sætra, H. S. (2021c). A framework for evaluating and disclosing the ESG related impacts of AI with the SDGs. *Sustainability, 13*, 8503.

Sætra, H. S. (2021d). Scaffolding human champions: AI as the more competent other. *Preprint*.

Sætra, H. S. (2022). A typology of AI applications in politics. In A. Visvizi & M. Bodziany (Eds.), *Artificial Intelligence and Its Context: Issues, Domains, Applications*. Cham: Springer.

Sætra, H. S., & Fosch-Villaronga, E. (2021). Research in AI has implications for society: How do we respond? *Morals & Machines, 1*(1), 60–73.

Sagers, C. (2019). Antitrust and Tech Monopoly: A General Introduction to Competition Problems in Big Data Platforms: Testimony Before the Committee on the Judiciary of the Ohio Senate. *Available at SSRN 3471823*.

Samui, P. (2019). *Application of artificial intelligence in geo-engineering*. Paper presented at the International Conference on Information Technology in Geo-Engineering.

Sattarov, F. (2019). *Power and Technology: A Philosophical and Ethical Analysis*. Lanham, MD: Rowman & Littlefield.

Sayer, A. (1992). *Method in Social Science: A Realist Approach*. London: Routledge.

Schwab, K. (2017). *The Fourth Industrial Revolution*. Redfern: Currency.

Sen, C. (2017, November 15th). The 'Big Five' Could Destroy the Tech Ecosystem. *Bloomberg*. Retrieved from https://www.bloomberg.com/opinion/articles/2017-11-15/the-big-five-could-destroy-the-tech-ecosystem.

Serrano, W. (2018). Digital systems in smart city and infrastructure: Digital as a service. *Smart Cities, 1*(1), 134–154.

Shapiro, A. (2017). Reform predictive policing. *Nature News, 541*(7638), 458.

Smith, R. E. (2019). *Rage Inside the Machine: The Prejudice of Algorithms, and How to Stop the Internet Making Bigots of Us All.* Nigel Newton: Bloomsbury Academic.

Solove, D. J. (2000). Privacy and power: Computer databases and metaphors for information privacy. *Stanford Law Review, 53*, 1393.

Sparrow, R. (2007). Killer robots. *Journal of Applied Philosophy, 24*(1), 62–77.

Sunstein, C. R. (2018). *# Republic: Divided Democracy in the Age of Social Media*. Princeton, NJ: Princeton University Press.

Sustainable development solutions network. (2021). Sustainable Development Report. Retrieved from https://www.sdgindex.org.

Thaler, R. H., & Sunstein, C. R. (2008). *Nudge: Improving Decisions About Health, Wealth, and Happiness*. New York: Yale University Press.

Toniolo, K., Masiero, E., Massaro, M., & Bagnoli, C. (2020). Sustainable business models and artificial intelligence: Opportunities and challenges. In *Knowledge, People, and Digital Transformation* (pp. 103–117), Cham: Springer.

Truby, J. (2020). Governing artificial intelligence to benefit the UN sustainable development goals. *Sustainable Development*. doi:10.1002/sd.2048.

Turkle, S. (2017). *Alone Together: Why We Expect More from Technology and Less from Each Other*. London: Hachette UK.

United Nations. (2015). Transforming our world: The 2030 Agenda for Sustainable Development. Division for Sustainable Development Goals: New York, NY, USA.

van Wynsberghe, A. (2021). Sustainable AI: AI for sustainability and the sustainability of AI. *AI and Ethics*, 1–6. doi:10.1007/s43681-021-00043-6.

Véliz, C. (2020). *Privacy Is Power*. London: Bantam Press.

Vinuesa, R., Azizpour, H., Leite, I., Balaam, M., Dignum, V., Domisch, S., … Nerini, F. F. (2020). The role of artificial intelligence in achieving the sustainable development goals. *Nature Communications*, 11(1), 1–10. doi:10.1038/s41467-019-14108-y.

World Resources Institute. (2021). We set the standards to measure and manage emissions. Retrieved from https://ghgprotocol.org.

Yeung, K. (2017). 'Hypernudge': Big Data as a mode of regulation by design. *Information, Communication & Society*, 20(1), 118–136. doi:10.1080/1369118X.2016.1186713.

Yigitcanlar, T., & Cugurullo, F. (2020). The sustainability of artificial intelligence: An urbanistic viewpoint from the lens of smart and sustainable cities. *Sustainability*, 12(20), 8548. doi:10.3390/su12208548.

Young, D. R., Fischer, H., Arterburn, D., Bessesen, D., Cromwell, L., Daley, M. F., … Horberg, M. A. (2018). Associations of overweight/obesity and socioeconomic status with hypertension prevalence across racial and ethnic groups. *The Journal of Clinical Hypertension*, 20(3), 532–540.

Zhang, D., Mishra, S., Brynjolfsson, E., Etchemendy, J., Ganguli, D., Grosz, B., … Perrault, R. (2021). *The AI Index 2021 Annual Report*. Retrieved from https://aiindex.stanford.edu/wp-content/uploads/2021/03/2021-AI-Index-Report_Master.pdf.

Zuboff, S. (2019). *The Age of Surveillance Capitalism:The Fight for a Human Future at the New Frontier of Power: Barack Obama's Books of 2019*. New York: PublicAffairs.

INDEX

Note: Italic page numbers refer to figures and page numbers followed by "n" denote endnotes.

Printed in the United States
by Baker & Taylor Publisher Services